Sexualising Society

Editor: Tracy Biram

Volume 386

independence
educational publishers

First published by Independence Educational Publishers

The Studio, High Green

Great Shelford

Cambridge CB22 5EG

England

© Independence 2021

Copyright

Photocopy licence

ISBN-13: 978 1 86168 844 6

Printed in Great Britain

Zenith Print Group

Contents

Chapter 1: Sexualisation

What is sexualisation? 1

The impact of over sexualisation of our teens 2

Sexualisation in gaming: advocacy and over-correction 5

Black women are constantly hypersexualised – it's time to stop fetishizing skin colour 7

Sexualised, mocked and fed to the wolves: why the Britney Spears story shames us all 9

Billie Eilish and the battle against sexualisation 11

These girls' stories of being sexualised underage proves how depressingly normal it is 12

'Cuties' calls out the hypersexualisation of young girls – and gets criticised 15

Why 'Cuties' does nothing to alter the Lolita infatuation 16

Why the sexual objectification of men isn't just a bit of fun 17

Schools urgently need to tackle rape culture by educating pupils about online world 19

Sex sells, right? 21

Sex in advertising: does it still sell? 24

German athlete Sarah Voss praised for wearing bodysuit to protest sexualisation of female gymnasts 26

Offence: sexualisation and objectification 27

Sexually objectifying women leads women to objectify themselves, and harms emotional well-being 28

Chapter 2: Pornography

What is porn? 30

Addicted to porn 31

Porn use is up, thanks to the pandemic 31

Porn and children: the facts 33

Is pornography to blame for the rise in rape culture? 35

We need to talk to our children about pornography – even if it makes us uncomfortable 37

Porn is not the root of all evil – yes, even when it comes to your children watching it behind your back 38

Key Facts 40

Glossary 41

Activities 42

Index 43

Acknowledgements 44

Introduction

Sexualising Society is Volume 386 in the **issues** series. The aim of the series is to offer current, diverse information about important issues in our world, from a UK perspective.

SEXUALISING SOCIETY

The sexualisation of society is apparent all around us. This book looks at sexualisation in advertising, in the entertainment industry and in pop culture in general. It considers how sexualisation is impacting our young people, particularly young girls. It also looks at the potential consequences of exposure to pornography and its prevalence in our world today.

OUR SOURCES

Titles in the **issues** series are designed to function as educational resource books, providing a balanced overview of a specific subject.

The information in our books is comprised of facts, articles and opinions from many different sources, including:

♦ Newspaper reports and opinion pieces

♦ Website factsheets

♦ Magazine and journal articles

♦ Statistics and surveys

♦ Government reports

♦ Literature from special interest groups.

A NOTE ON CRITICAL EVALUATION

Because the information reprinted here is from a number of different sources, readers should bear in mind the origin of the text and whether the source is likely to have a particular bias when presenting information (or when conducting their research). It is hoped that, as you read about the many aspects of the issues explored in this book, you will critically evaluate the information presented.

It is important that you decide whether you are being presented with facts or opinions. Does the writer give a biased or unbiased report? If an opinion is being expressed, do you agree with the writer? Is there potential bias to the 'facts' or statistics behind an article?

ASSIGNMENTS

In the back of this book, you will find a selection of assignments designed to help you engage with the articles you have been reading and to explore your own opinions. Some tasks will take longer than others and there is a mixture of design, writing and research-based activities that you can complete alone or in a group.

FURTHER RESEARCH

At the end of each article we have listed its source and a website that you can visit if you would like to conduct your own research. Please remember to critically evaluate any sources that you consult and consider whether the information you are viewing is accurate and unbiased.

Useful Websites

www.asa.org.uk

www.disrespectnobody.co.uk

www.independent.co.uk

www.jonnyshannon.com

www.mediatel.co.uk

www.metro.co.uk

www.npr.org

www.quillette.com

www.redbrick.me

www.safeschoolsallianceuk.net

www.scottishbordersrapecrisis.org.uk

www.shoutoutuk.org

www.telegraph.co.uk

www.theconversation.com

www.theguardian.com

www.thetab.com

www.wonderhatch.co.uk

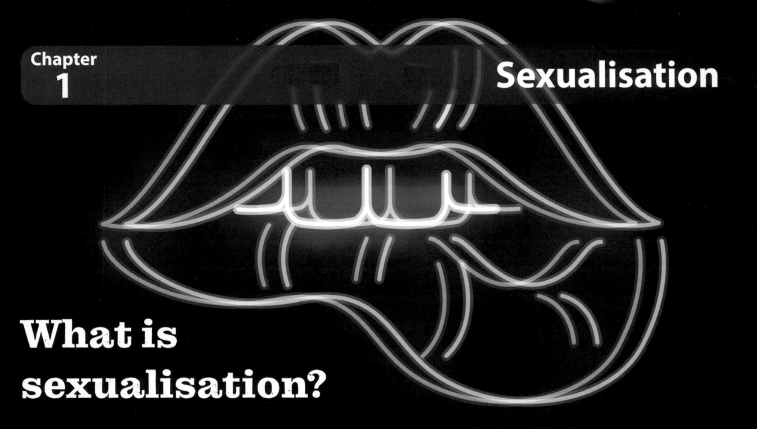

What is sexualisation?

Sexualisation can take lots of forms and can look different in different circumstances. We really like the definition that the American Psychological Association use. They say that sexualisation is when:

1. *a person's value comes only from their sexual appeal or behaviour, to the exclusion of other characteristics,* OR

2. *a person is held to a standard that equates physical attractiveness (narrowly defined) with being sexy,* OR

3. *a person is sexually objectified – that is, made into a thing for others' sexual use, rather than seen as a person with the capacity for independent action and decision making* OR

4. *sexuality is inappropriately imposed upon a person.*

If any one of these statements is true, then sexualisation is a problem but we typically see a number of these happen at the same time. For young people, the biggest problem is often number four - sexuality being imposed, inappropriately, on young people.

It's really important to remember that almost everyone has an interest in sex and has their own sexuality and that this is totally normal. Sexualisation is an issue because it imposes adult sexuality and harmful sexual stereotypes on young people. Zero Tolerance say that "increased self-objectification can impair girls' concentration, lead to depression, low self-esteem, eating disorders and diminished ability to form healthy sexual relationships when older. Boys may have distorted concepts and expectations about girls and women. Research has also discovered links between sexualisation of young people and violence – sexualisation can lead to more acceptable attitudes to violence, increased sexual harassment and to child sexual abuse."

Where does sexualisation of young people happen?

Everywhere! Sexualisation often happens at a societal level - this means that it's normal to see people, often women and girls, being sexualised in our daily lives, especially in the media. It's really common to see women being objectified and judged solely on their appearance in newspapers, magazines, on tv, in films, music videos and adverts.

So what does this mean?

Inappropriate sexualisation is a massive issue, not only because of all the negative effects we talked about above that it can have on individuals but because of the influence these images have on society. We asked young people in the Borders what messages they thought young girls and boys were growing up with because of sexualised images.

From our Scottish Young People Create Change (2016) event young people in the Borders commented on the 'dehumanisation' of women and girls stemming from 'sexualisation', objectifying and stereotyping of women. They felt there were expectations of how a girl or boy should behave.

Sexualisation is an issue for us because sexualised images show an incredibly tiny part of what human sexuality looks like but tell us that this is what it should be for everyone.

These messages tell us that everyone should look one way in order to be considered sexy or beautiful, they tell us that girls and boys, women and men must act and feel a certain way in order to be happy and they allow big companies to make lots of money from our sexuality. They rely on old fashioned and unrealistic gender stereotypes. They also promote unrealistic ideas of how bodies should look and how people should behave, particularly sexually. All of these issues can lead to big problems for individuals and for people in relationships.

2018

The impact of over sexualisation of our teens

By Jonny Shannon

How often have you heard someone in a TV or movie express surprise that another character didn't lose their virginity as a teenager? How many times have you seen older male characters hitting on much younger women? And how often have you looked at characters who are supposed to be teenage girls, but who look like they could easily be 25?

Sexualisation of teenagers in our media has always been a problem, but we're just now starting to realize the damage it causes. Read on to learn more about the impact of early sexualisation and what you can do to fight it.

Where sexualisation occurs

Sexualisation is so embedded in our media that many times, we may not even recognise it when it comes in front of us. Something like a pageant where young girls are dressed in suggestive costumes can start to impress that sexuality. And you don't have to look far in media to discover rampant over-sexualisation of young people.

How often have you seen a movie where a high school girl is dressed like a college student at a frat party? How about a TV scene where a teenager is ridiculed for not being sexually active yet? And of course, pornography is egregious in this area; millions of videos exist where an eighteen-year-old actress is made up to look much younger, implanting the idea that looking at fourteen-year-old girls in a sexual context is natural and appropriate.

Even female superheroes are often dressed in revealing clothing and move in suggestive ways. In fact, female characters move so differently than male characters that when the roles are reversed, they look absurd to us. And if you've ever looked at male versus female armour in an action video game, you'll notice that female armour has all sorts of "strategic" cutouts.

How early it begins

You would be shocked to discover how early the over-sexualisation of young people begins. For instance, if you have kids, how many times has someone looked at your infant son and said he's a stud? How many people have looked at your baby daughter and said she's already breaking hearts?

That messaging continues into when the child is old enough to understand some of what's being said. Thongs that say "Eye Candy" and "Wink Wink" are made in preschooler sizes. Dolls are shown in clothes like fishnet stockings, short skirts, and crop tops.

Why girls are targets

You may have noticed that we've been focusing on media that sexualises young girls. This isn't because boys aren't targets, too; in fact, we'll discuss later the harmful impact that this sexualisation has on boys. But girls tend to be the targets of direct sexualisation and the violence that comes from that.

Part of the reason girls tend to be targeted so much more often than boys is partly circular. We live in a society that tells us that women are little more than glorified sex objects. This leads movie and TV directors, video game developers, advertisers, clothing designers, toymakers, and everyone else to create more products based on this stereotype, which further promotes the sexualisation of children.

The impact of harmful gender stereotypes

This sexualisation is also the basis for many damaging gender stereotypes. Women and girls are stereotypically portrayed as being sexually available and subservient to the man in their life. Men are expected to be the stoic protectors; as we'll discuss in a moment, these stereotypes can not only damage relationships between men and women, but can also contribute to violence.

Children look to media and the adults around them as role models for how to act. When they see those hypersexual stereotypes, they assume that that's the accepted way to act and interact. And as they age, they continue receiving those messages from everything around them.

How stereotypes contribute to violence

Gender stereotypes are a large part of the reason that one in six women is sexually assaulted, one in four women experience intimate partner violence, and more than one and a half million women were the victims of violent crime last year. Women believe that intimate partner violence is normal and okay because they are told their role is subservient. They are told that their value lies in their sexuality and nothing more.

Men are taught that women are a commodity there for their enjoyment. Consent is not important because as the man, they have earned the right to female attention. When women don't conform to this passive sexuality, men are confused and angry, believing they have been cheated of something they have a right to.

Sexualisation and body image issues

This hypersexualisation also gives women unrealistic expectations about what their bodies should look like. Women in TV and movies have body proportions that are incredibly hard to achieve – tiny waistlines, big busts, and rounded hips. And these characters spend a huge amount of time discussing how they want to be even thinner, how their body is what gets them love, and how men are the central focus of their lives.

When you get into video games and toys, things get even worse. Free of the constraints of reality, designers can create women whose beauty ideal is literally impossible to achieve.

Facing all of these impossible role models, women and girls learn to see only the ways their bodies don't measure up.

Health risks of body image issues

If body image issues don't sound like that big a deal to you, you should know that every hour, another person dies from an eating disorder. At least 30 million people in the U.S. are living with an eating disorder. Eating disorders have the highest mortality rate of any mental illness, including depression.

And even outside eating disorders, women and girls may feel driven to do incredibly dangerous things to try to achieve the unrealistic beauty ideal they see in the media.

The Kylie Jenner challenge is the least of these worries. Women may engage in dangerous fad diets, undergo painful and expensive cosmetic surgery, and even turn to substance abuse as a way to cope with the self-loathing they feel for not measuring up in this one all important area.

Impact on adolescent boys

Now as we mentioned, teenage girls aren't the only ones affected by this hypersexualisation. Boys are taught from an early age that their role is as the stoic protector and the promiscuous stud. They are encouraged to shove down emotions, "take things like a man," and get laid as often as possible.

This culture of toxic masculinity can lead to suppressed rage causing men to lash out violently against women. Boys may feel pressured to start experimenting sexually before they're ready. And men, too, experience body image issues when they compare themselves to superheroes who have the proportions of a Dorito and the muscles of an early Captain America.

The impact of social media

All of the pressures we've discussed so far have been around for decades, and in some cases centuries. But in the last decade or so, a new player has come onto the scene: social media. Now young people see impossible standards every waking hour of the day and from people who they perceive to be peers.

Instagram models can portray an unrealistic standard that teenagers feel pressured to live up to. Angles, filters, and Photoshopping can do wonders, but these images are portrayed as reality. And adolescents are getting on social media and starting to absorb those damaging messages younger and younger these days.

7 ways to help decrease the sexualisation in media

1. Donate to change-making organizations

If you're like us, thinking about the rampant over-sexualisation of your children makes you angry. So what can you do to help? One of the best things you can do is to donate to charity organizations that focus on improving gender representation in media.

The Geena Davis Institute on Gender in Media works to engage, educate, and influence media producers to stop stereotyping female characters and portray diverse female characters instead. SPARK aims to create innovative solutions to combat sexualisation, objectification, and images of violence against women in media and society. And Together for Girls works to address harmful attitudes and social norms that condone violence against children.

2. Model healthy body positivity

The other huge thing you can do to combat this sexualization is to model healthy body positivity for the kids in your life. Don't talk about the weight you want to lose in front of them, and don't criticize yourself for not appealing to people because of how you look. Kids listen, and they mimic what they hear.

If kids ask you if something about their bodies is normal, unless it's a medical concern, tell them that it is a part of them and that makes it beautiful. Try to show them media that shows a diverse cast of characters who are treated in an age-appropriate manner. Most of all, treat your body as a wonderful vessel that carries you through life, not as a tool for winning love.

3. Buy age-appropriate clothing

When you're shopping for kids, it can be hard to avoid clothes that have an inappropriate sexual connotation. But work to find age-appropriate clothing, especially for girls. There's no reason a five-year-old should be in a bikini; they aren't old enough to make that decision about displaying their body in that way.

Don't allow little girls to wear makeup or outrageous earrings. These things are tools to make women appear more attractive, and these children are too young to worry about how attractive they are. Wait until they're old enough to make informed decisions about the way they present their bodies.

4. Push back against sexualization from outside sources

Many times, it can be easy to sit back and keep your mouth shut while outside sources sexualize children. Even if you disagree with what's being said, you may not want to cause a fuss. But we'd urge you to push back against those messages.

If someone comments that your baby is such a little heartbreaker, gently tell them that they're too young for those comments. Try to avoid media that overtly sexualises characters. And if your child does start asking questions about the way that certain characters are presented, be prepared to have a discussion with them about why it's fine to like that character without needing to be just like them.

5. Teach boys to respect women

A crucial step in breaking the cycle of sexualisation and gender stereotyping in the media is to teach boys to respect women. Those boys will grow up to be men, and those men will grow up to produce the next generation of media. If they're taught healthy values, they'll pass those along to the next generation.

Teach the little boys in your life emotional intelligence; allow them to cry, and teach them to process those emotions. Teach them by example and by what you tell them to treat girls the same way they'd treat other boys. And when they start getting old enough to date, teach them that consent is essential to every step of a healthy relationship.

6. Teach girls non-sexually-based self esteem

Likewise, teaching girls from a young age that their value lies in more than their sexuality will start to disrupt these stereotypes. By keeping them in age-appropriate clothing, you're already starting to break that stranglehold of over-sexualization. But it's important to teach them value outside of sexuality.

Tell the girls in your life that they are beautiful, yes. But also teach them that their bodies are marvelous vessels that can run and dance and sing and laugh. And as much as you tell them that they are beautiful, tell them that they're smart and powerful and brave and strong and that they can do anything.

7. Fight the sexualization of teens in media

Early sexualization of children and teenagers in media is a dangerous trend, and it can lead to violence, mental health issues, and eating disorders. But by changing the narrative, we can change this for future generations. Teach your kids that value lies outside sexuality, and donate to organisations working to change the message.

2020

Sexualisation in gaming: advocacy and over-correction

By Christopher J. Ferguson

Even before its April 2019 release, the eleventh instalment of the popular fighting game *Mortal Kombat* was generating waves for its presentation of female characters. But the grumblings are not what one might expect. After years of being criticized for sexualizing female characters, *Mortal Kombat* is now under fire from fans—including women—for not allowing the female characters to be sexy enough. Did *Mortal Kombat*'s developer overshoot the mark? Or are we beginning to see a reassessment of concerns that sexualised games are responsible for sexist attitudes toward women—an argument that increasingly became a mantra of progressive games criticism?

Historically, games have catered to male audiences, even as increasing numbers of women and girls have joined the ranks of gamers. Given the rapidly changing gamer demographic, it was perhaps inevitable that games would eventually come in for criticism for under-representing playable female characters, and for presenting them as hypersexualised images when they were available.

Much of this criticism was deserved, particularly the lack of alternative options featuring strong, less-sexualised playable characters. Indeed, I am on record advocating for stronger female characters in games. In recent years, the *Tomb Raider* reboot was praised for reimagining a less sexualised Lara Croft, and games such as *Alice: Madness Returns*, *Horizon Zero Dawn*, and *The Last of Us* have struck commercial gold with enticing, strong female leads. Commercially, *Mortal Kombat XI* will probably do just fine too. But why the sudden backlash against the covering up of the series' famously sexy females?

Part of it probably has to do with the specifics of *Mortal Kombat* as a series. Many of the games praised for promoting strong female leads were new franchises such as *The Last of Us* that didn't require developers to reimagine popular classics with an existing fan base. *Tomb Raider* is an exception, of course, but its reboot was a complete restart and felt like a fresh angle on a story that had grown stale. By contrast, *Mortal Kombat*'s redressing of its female characters may have been a shock particularly because some players feel that many of the male characters remain sexualised.

This backlash was foreseeable. Even as I supported the introduction of more strong women characters in games, I cautioned advocates against overplaying their hand. Just a few years ago, claims linking sexualised games to sexual assaults in real life were met with convincing criticism. The more subtle suggestion that sexualised games might cultivate sexism or misogyny have since become more common, particularly among cultural critics and some areas

of progressive games journalism, which have sacrificed a critical edge to the repetition of advocacy talking points with little concern for fact-checking or appropriate skepticism.

Cultivation theory suggests that, in the absence of other information, we develop beliefs or attitudes about the world based on media exposure. So, for instance, if a person regularly sees a lot of crime reported on the nightly news, they may come to believe that crime is more common than it actually is. However, even this fairly reasonable hypothesis has been maddeningly difficult to demonstrate. Is there any evidence that playing games such as *Grand Theft Auto* cultivates sexist attitudes in gamers?

A recent edition of scholar Christina Hoff-Sommers' vlog *Factual Feminist* poured cold water over this idea, noting that most social outcomes for women have improved, despite the vast popularity of sexualised games. But it's worth taking a closer look at the actual research base. As with most media effects fields, it's a mess, and advocates are making bold claims insufficiently supported by the available data.

A few years ago, much attention was given to a study conducted at Ohio State that looked at the impact of sexualised avatars on the acceptance of "rape myths." The study asked participants to move around a virtual world, but the exercise wasn't technically a video game. The study has often been described as showing that when women see their faces on sexualised avatars, they are more likely to accept rape myths. But this ignores one of the study's most interesting findings: rape myths among women were actually lowest among women who interacted as a sexualised avatar using a random face, and this is how most games such as *Grand Theft Auto* are actually played. Thus, this study could be used to suggest that playing most sexualized video games may reduce rather than increase rape myth acceptance, so long as women players avoid using their own faces on their avatars.

Another study, also conducted at Ohio State, exposed Italian boys to *Grand Theft Auto*, a non-sexualised violent game or a control violent game. No connection was found between game conditions and empathy toward female victims of violence. Nevertheless, the authors employed a dubious, complicated analysis to suggest that a reduced empathy effect was hidden in the results. Some outlets, like the ever-credulous *Time Magazine*, ate this story up. Unfortunately, it has been since discredited. A reanalysis I conducted with my colleague Brent Donnellan found that the study was not randomised, despite its authors claims to the contrary. All of the youngest boys ended up in the *Grand Theft Auto* cohort, with older boys more likely to end up in the non-sexist cohort. If random assignment had occurred, boys of different ages should be evenly spread throughout game conditions. But this is the opposite of what actually happened. In other words, age was conflated with game condition, a big problem since empathy tends to develop with age. Further, we found that even with that problem ignored, the analyses could not support even indirect links between *Grand Theft Auto* and sexism.

This study is a good example of what some call the Bullshit Asymmetry Factor. The study's claim to be randomised when in fact it was not should have been grounds for retraction.

However, its findings are still cited as if they provide evidence for effects. The Wikipedia page for sexism in video games, for instance, mentions only the original study, but fails to disclose that it was subsequently found to have fatal flaws.

Other recent studies have likewise failed to support the cultivation hypothesis. A 2015 study found no evidence that playing video games with sexual content is causally related to sexism later in life. Another recent study suggested that playing sexualised games might reduce rape myth acceptance over time. And a third found that cognitively demanding games, including sexualised games, could lead to decreased sexism. The problem is that research in this area tends to be inconsistent with studies that find effects and those that do not. Many studies also suffer from methodological flaws. On balance, this field is shaping up to be similar to the field dedicated to examining the effects of violence in video games. That is to say, high on rhetoric but ultimately low on evidence for effects in the real world.

None of this should discourage efforts to introduce non-sexualised female characters into games. However, advocates for this cause tend to make two mistakes. First, their claims about the causal relationship between gaming and real-world "harms" are unsupported by the current research evidence, and this misuse of data can reduce the credibility of an otherwise worthy cause. Second, there is a temptation to shift the focus from balance in game content to de facto censorship.

Which brings us to the question of whether it's simply good marketing to provide a variety of games for different audiences. Some producers, such as Sony, appear to accept that, at very least, they may experience some social backlash for sexualised images and are restricting content with this in mind. The trap into which both *Mortal Kombat* and Sony have fallen is that rather than providing a diversity of options, they decided to restrict the available options to those approved of by a narrow range of advocates. I suspect that developing games with strong non-sexualised characters will continue to be met with encouragement, whereas censoring existing game franchises will not. Or, put another way, there is room in the world for both *Grand Theft Auto 6* and *Horizon Zero Dawn 2*.

Ultimately, if game developers are producing games with more positive female characters, that is a positive development. However, they would also do well to avoid becoming merely an arm of an ideological advocacy agenda or exaggerating the impact their products have on consumers. Game companies which began at one extreme are now in danger of swinging to the other.

27 April 2019

Christopher J. Ferguson is a professor of psychology at Stetson University in Florida. He is author of *Moral Combat: Why the War on Violent Video Games is Wrong* and the Renaissance mystery novel *Suicide Kings*. You can follow him on Twitter @CJFerguson1111

Black women are constantly hypersexualised – it's time to stop fetishising skin colour

Historically, black women's bodies are fair game.

By Natalie Morris

We are hypersexualised from an alarmingly young age and there is a collective tendency to dissect us into nothing more than body parts and sexual acts.

From music videos to movies to images of celebrities – the mainstream media perpetuates this obsession with the black, female form – at the expense of acknowledging us as human beings with brains and hearts and opinions, as well as tits and ass.

Despite being the least successful group on dating apps, black women are widely desired on the basis of archaic, offensive sexual stereotypes.

It's a form of sexual racism, and it needs to stop.

Fetishisation means to form an obsessive, sexual connection based on a particular feature or item – and racial fetishism is where that connection is based on person's race or ethnic group.

You know what the stereotypes are. That black women are 'wild' in bed, aggressively dominant sexually, promiscuous, always up for it.

They are beliefs that derive from long-standing stereotypes about black women – namely the Jezebel stereotype – and they are contrasted by images of the purity and self-control of white women.

The inference is that black women are the type you can enjoy in the bedroom, but not necessarily bring home to your mum.

It's a trope that began in slavery in the 1800s, where black, female slaves were reduced to nothing more than 'breeders', and were frequently raped by slave owners. But the legacy of this dehumanising behaviour still lingers today.

Of course, this isn't a view shared by everyone. Plenty of people are able to see through these stereotypes for what they really are – prejudiced, racist slurs.

But the anecdotal evidence of how often black women are approached with propositions based solely on sexual stereotypes, suggests it is still a worryingly common belief. It isn't only black women who are subject to sexual racism. It is something faced by all women of colour.

Whether you're Asian, Hispanic, mixed-race, or, basically, any variation of not-white, it seems there are certain sexual assumptions people will make based on your skin colour.

Asian women are submissive, Latina women are feisty, black women are easy.

And, in other parts of the world, white women are also fetishised because of their skin tone and appearance.

In the UK it manifests in the language used to describe women of colour.

Skin tone is often equated to something edible. We are 'caramel', 'chocolate', 'mocha'. The message is clear – we are something to be devoured, our sole purpose is to provide pleasure through consumption.

But sexual proclivity has nothing to do with skin tone, or race. How could it?

What's really going on here is projection. People are projecting their racial prejudices onto women in the form of fetishisation. It's more widespread than you might think, and more often than not, it's entirely unconscious.

Student activists Sara, Sarah and Alison, have decided something needs to be done to raise awareness about the damaging effects of racial hypersexualisation.

They started the #F*ckYourFetish campaign because they were tired of people making assumptions about their sexuality based on their race. What they want is to hold people to account.

'From being sexually harassed to seeing dating sites allowing users to promote their fetishes, we see women of colour being reduced to stereotypes everywhere,' they tell Metro.co.uk.

'The campaign was necessary because of the way in which this problem has been normalised in society.

'As women, we often don't even realise that we are being racially sexualised and that is problematic. In the same way, sometimes men can't see its harmful effects, especially when they are the ones perpetuating it.'

The girls, who are all in sixth form together, hijacked advertising space on the London Underground to promote their campaign.

Predictably, they have received backlash from the #NotAllMen brigade, but they say it's vital that everyone acknowledges and understands what they're trying to achieve.

'In day-to-day interactions, women are fetishised through the concept of sexual "preferences". We believe it happens because some men think it's a compliment and a way to appease their desires,' they explain.

'Words like exotic are thrown around, as such, women of colour become objects for gratification rather than women with minds. Overall, it feeds into a system that keeps women subordinate.'

Sarah, Sara and Alison are Asian, Afro-Latina, and black African, respectively. They are still teenagers, and already they have a disturbing amount of experience of being racially fetishised.

'For me, hypersexualisation has been an undercurrent for as long as I can remember,' explains Alison.

'I was always told to not dress "fast", and that wearing makeup would make me look "ready". I often asked, "ready for what?" Until it clicked. Ready for sex.

'It infects our households, and our mothers dress us to make sure no one sexualises us for spaghetti straps on dresses, or for showing our legs, or having a pair of jeans that over emphasises the bottom.

Sara's experience as an Afro-Latina has been slightly different.

'For me, racialised hypersexualisation is often linguistically focused,' says Sara.

'As soon as people learn that I am from Dominican Republic, their response is to call me, "Mamasita". I am called, the "lightskin Latina with the big back", or "The Spanish girl" – there's so much more to me, and I find it so reductive.'

'Society needs to realise that objectifying and sexualising women is not okay,' explain the campaigners.

'This change needs to take place in people's mindsets where they finally view women as equals. So men need to stop basing their "type" on their racial preferences.

'Stop the catcalling and the wolf-whistling, stop the harassment and stop controlling women.'

It's disheartening that today's sixth form students are still facing these archaic stereotypes about sex. But awareness is the first step in changing behaviours, and campaigns like this can be the starting point.

Experiencing racial fetishisation is incredibly hurtful and demeaning.

Whether it's offensive comments on dating apps, presumptuous behaviour on first dates, or a reluctance to take things beyond the bedroom – fetishisation based on race isn't merely an expression of sexual preference, it's racism.

By casting women of colour in certain sexual roles, before understanding anything about them beyond their appearance, we make it clear that their only value is that of a sexual commodity.

Non-white women are more than simply sexual objects – it seems ludicrous to have to say that, and most of us know this consciously.

It's the unconscious that potentially needs examining – particularly when it comes to sexual preferences and inherent assumptions.

8 January 2019

Sexualised, mocked and fed to the wolves: why the Britney Spears story shames us all

As new documentary Framing Britney makes clear, the pop star was cruelly vilified from an early age. Is so much different today?

By Kate Solomon

On 7 February, as the Super Bowl kicked off in the US and most of the UK lay sleeping, a hashtag overwhelmed the trending topics on Twitter. Nothing to do with sports or slumber, it read in fervent capitals WE ARE SORRY BRITNEY.

Casual fans had settled in to watch the New York Times' documentary *Framing Britney Spears*, perhaps hoping for a bit of nostalgia, a touch of drama and some chance to remind themselves of the hectic period of Spears' life when she was never off the front pages for all the wrong reasons. Instead, viewers were forced to reckon with their own role in the star's mistreatment at the hands of the media, her family, the legal system and popular culture as a whole.

If you were to write a guide on how not to interview a teenage girl, where would you start? Would you perhaps begin by insisting that the septuagenarian interviewer not ask their prepubescent subject if he could be her boyfriend? Would you suggest that, maybe, asking an 18-year-old girl about the status of her virginity should be off limits?

Perhaps you'd check over your questions beforehand and take out any that make reference to a teenager's breasts. If only this guide had existed 20 years ago, we could have stemmed at least some of the incessant hypocrisy and misogyny that flowed towards Spears.

Age 11, after starring in The All-New Mickey Mouse Club, she fended off *Starsearch* host Ed McMahon's comedic but clearly still uncomfortable advances with carefully

inoffensive responses that any woman who's had to extricate themselves from unwanted attention will recognise.

"Well, that depends," she croaks with a frown when he asks if he can be her boyfriend; the crowd chuckles. During her relationship with Justin Timberlake between 1998 and 2002, the question of whether the two had slept together repeatedly came up – in *Framing Britney Spears*, she's asked in the middle of a press conference whether or not she is a virgin. Timberlake will later use his claim that they slept together as part of the launch of his solo career.

These lines of questioning would not fly today, not without uproar or, hopefully, the star feeling like she can push back and refuse to answer at the very least. But Britney was, in many ways, a trailblazer in this instance. She broke out during a period where boy bands ruled the roost; there were very few young, female stars who achieved the level of success that she did in the late 1990s. As someone releasing pure pop music she wasn't taken seriously as an artist, dismissed as disposable music for girls and eye-candy for boys.

But as the documentary makes clear, Britney had a great deal of control over her artistic choices in the early days, and she always pushed back against the image of the perfect all-American girl. It was her idea, for instance, to wear school uniform in the iconic video for her debut 1998 single ...*Baby One More Time* – but if you're seen as the perfect specimen of girlhood, there's absolutely no way that you can win.

The Madonna/Whore hypocrisy has never been so overt as in the media's treatment of Britney Spears in the early 2000s. In psychology, Sigmund Freud coined the term Madonna-Whore Complex to describe men who see women only as virginal and pure or sexual and debased. This is how popular culture saw Britney Spears: the good girl who they could not condone being a sexual being, even while constantly sexualising her.

It wasn't just male interviewers who fed into it. The documentary includes footage of Britney Spears on *Dateline* in 2003, presented by Diane Sawyer. Sawyer manages to pester a 21-year-old Spears for intimate details of her sex life, tell her a Governor's wife wants to shoot her for being a bad role model and insinuate that Spears has no one to blame but herself for the backlash after she and Timberlake broke up.

Timberlake, incidentally, emerges unscathed, despite gleefully spilling details of their intimate sexual moments and making an extremely creepy music video where he breaks into a Spears-lookalike's house, spies on her in the shower then has revenge sex on her bed. Interesting to compare this to how he was treated in the aftermath of the Superbowl in 2004, when he exposed Janet Jackson's nipple in front of America: she was shamed into years of reclusion, he suffered no consequences of note.

The documentary makes plain the toll that all of this has taken on Spears even before it reaches the truly upsetting events of 2007. In the interviews she did as a bright-eyed teen she is confident, sure of herself and her mind – by 2003, she is cautious. She looks tired, her make-up heavily and hastily applied, her pleasant facade dissolving into tears as the weight of the inappropriate questioning piles up. If you've ever perused Spears' Instagram account you'll recognise the brittle, trapped look in her eye as she twirls and dances in low-resolution. It sometimes feels as though she is begging us to believe she is OK.

All the misogynistic pearl-clutching ignored the fact that Spears was simply holding a mirror up to adolescent girlhood. It's not unusual for teens to hike their skirts up and unbutton their school shirts as low as they can get away with; it's not a heinous crime for teens to make out with each other, to explore their bodies as they age into maturity. Britney Spears reflected this back at us, sometimes literally (as with the *Baby One More Time* video and the mournful ballad *Not A Girl Not Yet A Woman*) and sometimes simply by being herself.

Of course, this was a large part of the reason that teenagers related to and adored Britney Spears. In particular, she appealed to LGBTQ+ youths who were struggling to find their footing in the world. "I heard this story that didn't make it in the film," director Samantha Stack told Queerty. She referenced some cut interview footage with Britney's long-time assistant and friend Felicia Culotta. "Felicia said Britney was judged for being herself. So if you were judged for being yourself, you related to her. She related to you."

In 2007, Spears' personal life descended into tabloid fodder. She was constantly hounded by paparazzi as public appetite for the fallout of her mental health issues reached fever pitch. The infamous head-shaving of 2007 is contextualised by the bitter custody battle that was raging between Spears and her one-time husband Kevin Federline. She was stuck in a vicious circle: she couldn't escape the paparazzi but to avoid them meant being a prisoner in her own home.

The more she was seen, the more the public wanted to see her; the more chaotic her life became, the more the paparazzi goaded her toward breaking point. Her troubles were breathlessly reported, her struggles with her mental health becoming a punchline for talkshow hosts and quiz show rounds. Spears ended up being hospitalised for a spell; and this is when her father took over her affairs.

Her queer fans are responsible, in large part, for the Free Britney movement that arguably spurred *Framing Britney Spears* into existence. Since 2007, Spears has been under a conservatorship that means her father controls her finances, her work and most aspects of her life. The conservatorship is contentious alone – it's a legal tool usually used to hand control of an individual's affairs over when they are suffering mind-altering conditions like dementia, as they approach the end of their lives. People don't get out of conservatorships: they die.

Jamie Spears does not come off well in the new documentary; he is described as financially anxious in the way that anyone who has come from nothing and briefly had a lot seems to be. Once you have money, you don't want to lose it: Jamie Spears' money comes from his daughter and her money comes from being Britney Spears. Their relationship is not considered close. Earlier this year Britney petitioned the courts to allow her to remove her father from her conservatorship, to allow a bank to manage her finances instead.

The Free Britney movement is a collective of fans who picket outside the courts and work online to raise awareness of the trap that they feel that Britney Spears is currently in. In fact, it's impossible to know what situation Spears is truly in at the moment. She has not given an interview for many years. Most people in her current inner circle refused to speak to the documentary makers. Her current staff and her family declined to participate: instead we have insight from her former assistant, a former choreographer, her agent and the head of marketing at her first label, as well as some paparazzi and tabloid editors. Britney herself could not be reached.

The one glimpse any of us have into her life as it is, is via her Instagram account on which she showcases the meditative quality of kinetic sand, dance moves, flowers, inspirational quotes and many and varied photographs of baths. Some have read into her posts, claiming there are coded cries for help amid the rampant emoji. She seems fragile but happy; just getting on with the business of being herself, enjoying her indefinite hiatus from popstar life.

The story is far from at its end, but we are lucky that the wringer we put Britney Spears through did not have a more tragic outcome. Others have not been so lucky: Amy Winehouse, who would no doubt hate to be compared to Britney, nevertheless has a lot in common with her. She, too, had a withholding father who ended up in charge of her affairs; few close friends; very public mental health issues; incessant press attention and cruel jokes made at the expense of her very serious problems.

Though we have begun to care for our young artists more, there are still ways that they are hounded and damaged by society and our actions within them: just look at Little Mix's Jesy Nelson, who was moved to make an entire documentary about the ways that being in the public eye has impacted her mental health, before leaving her girl group altogether.

As traditional media falls in influence and we gain more individual and collective power through social media, it's on all of us to learn from the many awful mistakes made with Britney Spears, to interrogate how we treat women in the public eye and to consider our own roles in these too-often tragic stories. We want our celebrities to be Teflon, for nothing we think or say to stick to them, but that simply isn't the case.

In 20 years, if someone makes another documentary about another now-starlet, would our own behaviour pass muster? Right now, I doubt it.

16 February 2021

Billie Eilish and the battle against sexualisation

Life & Style Writer Amy Larsen examines Eilish's unique style in light of the sexualisation of young celebrities.

By Amy Larsen, 1st year English Literature student

Billie Eilish took home four Grammys at the recent 2020 awards show, making her the second artist ever to win all four of these categories in one night. As a young artist Eilish has already achieved so much in her career, with her album, 'When We All Fall Asleep, Where Do We Go?' remaining at number 1 in the Official Charts for 3 weeks. Eilish writes and records music with her brother Finneas O'Connell and rose to fame after 'Ocean Eyes' was uploaded to SoundCloud and went viral in 2015. Eilish was just 14 at the time.

As a result of her success, Eilish has grown up in the public eye and only recently turned 18. Fame and success brings with it judgement, criticism and in many cases trolling online. Despite her undoubted talent as an artist, Billie Eilish is by no means immune to this type of judgement and has been subjected to sexualisation. Eilish is known for her outlandish and oversized clothing but in June 2019, whilst at a meet and greet before her show, she wore a tank top and was photographed by a fan. This picture started trending and memes sexualising the young singer on social media soon followed. When asked about it in an Elle interview Eilish recalled how her 'boobs were trending on Twitter!'.

Although Eilish was under the age of 18 at the time, the magazine notes how 'even CNN wrote a story about Eilish's boobs'. Billie went on to discuss her fashion choices and how she covers her body in order to avoid judgement. Her bold fashion and deliberate decision to wear oversized clothes appear to be a reaction to and rejection of this type of sexualisation.

> *"Her most recent posts display her neon green hair, long, black acrylic nails and oversized clothes."*

Billie Eilish also spoke about her style in a 2019 interview with Vogue Australia and discussed why she chooses to wear baggy clothes, stating it 'gives nobody the opportunity to judge what your body looks like'. Eilish is completely aware of the sexualisation of young celebrities and her desire to hide her body in order to avoid this says something deeply troubling about our society. Eilish went on to describe fashion as her 'security blanket' and a way that she feels able to express herself without having to actually say anything. In a 2017 interview with Vanity Fair Eilish was asked to describe her style in three words and replied simply, 'judge me please'. This can be viewed as a clear indicator that Eilish's fashion choices are deliberately unique and eye-catching. Scrolling through her Instagram account showcases this striking style. Her most recent posts display her neon green hair, long, black acrylic nails and oversized clothes, every outfit covered in layers of chains and jewellery. Eilish's style can be viewed as an expression of her individuality and a rejection of her sexualisation. It

portrays an inspiring message to her 54.3 million followers, particularly fellow teens, as Eilish wears what she wants and doesn't care what anyone has to say about it.

> *"The sexualisation of young celebrities is an issue that needs to be addressed."*

Billie Eilish is not the only young celebrity to be subjected to sexualisation. Refinery29 noted how the love life of 'Stranger Things' actress, Millie Bobby Brown, was speculated about in the media when she was just 13 years of age. They also referenced Natalie Portman's experience which she discussed at the 2018 Women's March in light of the #MeToo campaign. Portman recalled how men would talk about her breasts before she was even a teenager. Additionally, actress, Emma Watson gave a speech to the United Nations in 2014 in which she described being sexualised at age 14 during the fame of the Harry Potter films. Young, male celebrities are not immune to this type of judgement. Justin Bieber experienced extreme popularity after his hit song 'Baby' was released 10 years ago, when he was 16 years old and singer Sinead O'Connor, stated that Bieber was exploited and 'sold on his sexuality'.

The sexualisation of young celebrities is an issue that needs to be addressed. Despite the progress caused by movements such as the #MeToo campaign and the discussions that have followed, there is still much room for improvement.

6 March 2020

These girls' stories of being sexualised underage proves how depressingly normal it is

'Every girl has a story like this'.

By Lydia Venn

Growing up as a girl, there is one thing that unites us all – our experiences of sexism at a very young age. Being told our skirts are a distraction for male teachers, being shouted at from a van whilst on a jog or being teased for the size of our boobs. Ask any woman you know and they will relate to at least one of these experiences.

When I reached out to the women in my life, I was inundated with examples of everyday sexism and sexualisation of girls who have stories from as young as 11-years-old. And what's even worse is many of them were so similar and were things we'd got so used to happening that we've accepted them as the normal rite of passage of being a teenage girl.

These experiences are not what we should all have in common and yet they are so prevalent in our lives. The policing of our bodies and clothing comes from our teachers, parents, friends and sometimes even ourselves as a result of internalised misogyny.

The stories I collected from a variety of young women showed that these early encounters of sexualisation are more than just being told our skirt is too short (although that is very often the case). The stories stretch across every moment of our lives from hobbies, to working out, to your first job at the local sandwich shop, to simply walking down the road.

These are just some real life examples of times girls were sexualised at a young age:

School

"I remember being called a porn star when I was in year seven by the boys at my school because my boobs developed early. I was so confused because obviously I couldn't do anything about it but the boys just seemed to sexualise them so much, which I now realise was actually really off putting and made me self conscious.

"I remember being so embarrassed and not telling anybody that they were saying it, and all my friends just finding it funny when in reality it made my body become sexualised before I had even hit puberty properly.

"I remember being in like year eight or nine and a guy photoshopped my face onto like a porn photo. Loads of my mates messaged saying 'I can't believe you sent him that pic' and obviously I denied it as I didn't, but didn't really think much of that until I was older! The guy messaged me apologising but I still think it's mad that he did that." Gemma

"At my boarding school, it was against school rules to wear a coloured bra because the pink straps were too distracting. So we'd wear black, white and skin coloured and when that apparently became too distracting, it was against the rules to have straps showing unless in your boarding house and teachers would send girls to the principa's office if their straps were showing." Vicki

"My sixth form history teacher would call me 'Love' and nobody else. My whole class picked up on it basically straight away and he stopped… I think he meant it in a 'nice' way as I was going off to do history at uni but yeah, a bit weird." Susie

"Teachers' over use of the phrase 'that's not very lady like'." Lucy

"I think young girls being told they're bossy instead of just leaders, never really heard the boys in school get called bossy." Liv

"I remember in my physics class a female student was putting on lipgloss and the male teacher told her 'Stop that! It's tempting'." Funmi

"I used to wear TWO BRAS to school because I was scared boys would say my boobs were small otherwise." Maddy

"It's so toxic how girls are programmed to take responsibility for men's actions. A 60-year-old teacher at my school had a relationship with a 17-year-old pupil and so many of my friends blamed her and called her a slut and his wife defended him saying the girl was the predator and had tempted him." Emily

"I always had big boobs growing up and used to get bullied mercilessly for it. I got called 'melons' every day between the ages of 12 and 16. So I was led to believe I was unattractive and fat. I wanted a breast reduction for my 16th." Molly

"I remember one non-school uniform day in year seven, I wore this red nautical playsuit (in hindsight, not cute, but I LOVED it) and on the way to my next class a boy shouted 'slut' at me. When I told a teacher passing by, she told me that it was probably the way I was dressed." Kea

School skirts (yes they need their own category)

"When I was at school, I would always have teachers (male and female) telling me to pull my skirt down and had a science teacher once tell me to sit on a chair as a 'lady' otherwise it would distract the male teachers (I was sat with my legs over the arm rest)." Georgia

"I went to an all girls school year seven to year 11 and there was a male teacher who used to carry round a ruler to measure our skirts to make sure they weren't distracting if they were too short." Alice

Being sexualised doesn't end when you grow up.

"When I started an all girls secondary school we were told we weren't allowed to wear our P.E. skorts around school unless we put tracksuit bottoms over the top or wear shorts on non uniform day because it was 'distracting'.

"Since other girls saw the skorts in P.E. lessons it can't have been about distracting our fellow pupils so the only logical assumption is that they thought we, at 11, would distract our teachers with our legs. Very victim-blamey because if a 30-year-old teacher is driven to distraction by a pubescent child's legs then that is very much their problem." Caitlin

"A female teacher once told my 14-year-old self that my skirt was too short and made me pull it down in front of an entire canteen of students." Sapphire

"Teachers would measure our skirts with rulers. I was tall so they always slut-shamed me and all the other tall girls would have to wear super long skirts to appease the puritans." Funmi

"All the girls in my year got given detention for having too short skirts at our Catholic school because it was distracting for the boys and male teachers." Eirian

"I remember at the start of year 10 my skirt was too small and therefore quite short and one of my friends said something like 'I can't believe you want to look like one of those sluts'." Caitlin

Family

"I'm 21 and my mum will say my top is too revealing if I'm showing a slight bit of cleavage and that I should cover up so I don't get stared at." Claudia

"I remember at 15 my dad told me to take down a picture off Instagram because I 'looked like a prostitute'." Alice

"My sister in law, who wasn't married to my brother at the time, told me to change my bra because you could see it slightly through the top I was wearing. What has it got to do with anyone what fucking bra I choose to wear? – I was 14 at the time." Beth

"Wearing anything short when you were younger whether that's a skirt or shorts and your mum or someone older saying 'you're not wearing that out' – when there's literal men on the street with their tops off." Lucy

Work

"I worked at a golf club near my home. There was at a themed night and we had a DJ in – he made comments about how my shirt would take a man's eye out (it was a normal button shirt) and then made a comment about my school shoes like how I was still at school.

"I didn't feel comfortable working there anymore and the golf club were shocking when dealing with it. They spoke to him about the comments on the shift but refused to ban him from the club, they said he wasn't actually directly employed by them, it was whoever the DJ company wanted to send." Georgia

"I worked at this little shop from age 13 – 16 every Saturday morning, and the amount of grim comments I'd get from like old men or like workmen when I was making them sandwiches was obscene.

"This one guy used to always ask me for a kiss with his sandwich and make comments about my body when I'd turn around, and ask what time I'd finish. I was 13 so didn't know how to tell him to piss off whilst still being polite? The boss was a family friend and used to laugh and go with it because he didn't want to offend the customers.

"Most of the time they didn't know how old I was, but like that's no excuse?? I always got my dad to pick me up even though I only lived a five minute walk away." Tiffany

"I worked in a kitchen around men all the time who used to be predatory on me and the other girls." Beth

Exercise

"Don't even get me started on my mum, she's always trying to police my outfits, such as my workout outfit I've been wearing at home (which obvs no one is seeing) and how it's too revealing 'who are you trying to impress'". Alice

"You can imagine what it was like when I started playing water polo at 13… Obviously that was for more attention and to show my body off in a swimming costume." Alice

"Even now I won't go for a run in just a sports bra and leggings, I have to put on a top, because I don't want the risk." Rachel

"Honestly I'm still low key scared to go running because without fail I'll either get cat called or called a fat bitch, or more likely both." Sophia

Literally just walking around

"Sometimes these gross guys will catcall you and follow up with racial slurs if you don't answer them." Funmi

"I was 14-years-old and was walking with a friend down a main road, we were both wearing shorts. We got tooted and

I remember feeling really proud, but now looking back on it, it's weird that a grown adult honked at two children." Rachel

"Shouting at you from cars/vans is a classic. It's so jarring. You could be having an amazing day and then it's just dampened down." Funmi

Driving Lessons

"When I was learning to drive age 17 I had this instructor who was everything your parents tell you to look out for. When I think back to it now I feel so uncomfortable and annoyed I didn't say anything.

"He was a massive creep and would talk about sex in front of me all the time, comment on the length of my skirt, and would ask really inappropriate questions about me and my boyfriend's sex life.

"At the time I would just laugh it off and play along because I was scared. I never said anything to the driving company or my parents because I was both worried he would find out it came from me.

"And I was worried he would lose his job…which is so mad now I look back on it because why did I feel bad about some absolute creep losing his job when he almost definitely being a perv to other girls learning to drive just like me. I felt like I shouldn't cause a scene, and that it was wrong to stand up for myself and call it out – now I look back on it I really wish I had." Lucy

June 2020

'Cuties' calls out the hypersexualisation of young girls – and gets criticised

By Rebecca Rosman

The French film, *Cuties*, is being praised for its critique of the hypersexualisation of young girls - and the consequences of that – as they rush to become adults in the age of social media.

It began several years ago when filmmaker Maimouna Doucouré was at a neighborhood gathering and her jaw dropped. A group of young girls in revealing outfits came out on a stage and performed a choreographed routine.

Doucouré says they couldn't have been more than 11 years old.

"And they were dancing very sensually, sexually and I was very disturbed about what I was seeing."

But instead of passing judgment, the self-taught writer and filmmaker says she wanted to understand what she was seeing. She dove into research, interviewing more than one hundred adolescent girls over the course of a year and a half.

"It's a period [that's] very specific," Doucouré says, "where you are not any more totally a child and you are not an adult. You are looking for yourself and everything is changing very fast."

Doucouré combines her findings with elements of her own upbringing in her first feature length film, *Cuties*.

It's about what it means to be an adolescent girl in the age of TikTok and Instagram, where 'likes' have become the currency of self-esteem and keeping kids away from anything on the Internet is near impossible.

The film is told from the perspective of 11-year-old Amy who, like Doucouré, is the daughter of Muslim Senegalese immigrants growing up in northeast Paris.

Amy is unimpressed by the traditional path for women laid out by the matriarchs in her family.

As her strict Grand-Aunt tries to groom her to become a wife and mother, Amy watches her own mom struggle to hide tears when she gets a call from her husband in Senegal. As is tradition for many men there, he's taken a second wife.

To escape the drama playing out at home, Amy befriends a group of popular girls at school who have formed a dance troop called 'Les Mignonnes' or 'the Cuties.'

Amy spends hours nailing down choreography to provocative music videos so she can impress her new friends.

Filmmaker Doucouré says social media adds a layer of complexity to what it means to be an adolescent in 2020.

"Today you have that exposition of your body on social media," Doucouré says, "and you also have this big competition of finding 'likes' and followers and that is for me a new kind of finding love."

The film provokes many questions, but doesn't provide many answers. And that's the intention, says French film critic Jennifer Padjemi, who says it's also important that *Cuties* was made by a woman who comes from the same background and culture as her characters.

"It's really important to have more coming of age movies in France in general and not with only white casts," Padjemi says, "because it's important to represent children of every background because even if we live the same way we don't have the same cultural path and it's really important to see this specific age between childhood and teenage-hood and I hope Maimouna open[s] the door for other movies like this."

That door almost didn't open.

Even though *Cuties* has received widespread acclaim in France and won a Sundance award, a publicity gaffe from its US distributor, Netflix, almost cost the movie its reputation.

After Netflix published a marketing poster showing the 'Cuties' twerking in revealing cheerleading outfits without any context, an online petition calling for the cancellation of the US release received more than 140 thousand signatures.

Doucouré was accused, on social media, of being a paedophile and even received death threats.

She says she hopes those who signed the petition will watch the film.

"And after that, they will see that we have the same fight and we are all together about that issue of hypersexualisation of our children and protect our children."

In the end, Doucouré says her film is about a choice.

"The choice [of] who we want to become, who we want to really become and as a child, take the time to be a child. Keep that innocence to grow up in our society."

6 September 2020

Objectified women

Sexual objectification typically takes one of two forms. In the first, eroticised depictions of female bodies present women as mere resources – nothing more than "eye candy" for male sexual gratification. Such portrayals encourage more general exploitative attitudes towards women. By implicitly denying women's agency, they appear to legitimise coercive behaviour and in extreme cases sexual violence.

In the second, women's agency is not ignored but actively recruited for oppressive purposes. In this case, rather than reducing women to the status of mere resources, the objectifying content has the effect of scripting their behaviour – tacitly promoting norms and stereotypes of conduct geared to the sexual gratification of men. Women are invited to play along with the roles allotted to them, consenting to, and even enthusiastically embracing, treatment that is in reality exploitative. Objectification in this sense works by colonising women's identities. It is subtly ideological rather than brutally coercive.

Flipping the male gaze

So, what of the objectification of men, and the existence of an apparent double standard?

If we only think in terms of the first form of objectification, and the consumption of "eye candy", we are likely to conclude that the sexual objectification of men is a relatively trivial matter. Prevailing physical, political and economic power inequalities are such that in practice a man's agency is much less likely than a woman's to be overridden.

Consequently, the objectification of men is much less likely to result in sexual violence. To this extent, a double standard might be thought tolerable.

However, in relation to the second form of objectification – where damaging norms and stereotypes are promoted and internalised – it's difficult to defend the double standard.

There seems to be no good reason to think that men are any less suggestible and compliant than women are when it comes to "normalising" media representations. Young and impressionable men in particular may be as biddable and eager to play along as their female counterparts.

Consider the way men are presented on programmes such as ITV's *Love Island*. The producers of the programme stress that it does not pretend to hold a mirror up to life, but provides an idealised and in their own words "aspirational" portrayal. But when narcissism, individualism, materialism and manipulation are presented as aspirational, audiences are likely to find themselves emulating behaviour that is incompatible with healthy relationships and a fulfilling life.

Audience appetites

Objectifying media content is sometimes defended on the basis that it doesn't play an ideological role but only caters to the preexisting appetites of its audience. However, even in much more neutral contexts, such as fashion and car magazines, such arguments don't stand up. It is no doubt true that magazines are usually read by people who have a preexisting interest in their content. But most people will be familiar with the experience of picking up a magazine and finding they have suddenly developed a keen interest in which £200,000 supercar is really most desirable. If it didn't work that way, no one would loan £200,000 supercars to journalists.

Clearly, media representations do far more than cater to preexisting appetites. They actively shape what we aspire to, what we are prepared to consent to, and the ways we spend our time and money in pursuit of what we (consequently) want. Advertising, entertainment and news media play a significant ideological role in our lives. Power, as Foucault observed, is insidious and productive. It typically operates not by overt interdiction or coercion, but by creatively and "consensually" shaping our selfconceptions and (thereby) our views of what is normal and desirable.

So, we should be concerned about the sexual objectification of men. The real issue though is not women's responses to eroticised drama, nor the feelings of the male actors involved, nor (realistically) the possibility that such scenes might lead to a significant rise in sexual violence against men. The issue is that the ideological scripting of men's behaviour is coming to be as all-pervasive as the ideological scripting of women's behaviour.

At the same time as young men are being encouraged to be increasingly narcissistic and materialistic, they are experiencing unprecedented levels of perfectionism-driven social anxiety and mental illness. This is perhaps understandable, given that they are being bombarded with a vastly greater quantity and intensity of objectifying media content than previous generations ever had to contend with.

18 September 2018

Schools urgently need to tackle rape culture by educating pupils about online world

An article from The Conversation

THE CONVERSATION

By Tanya Horeck, Jessica Ringrose, Kaitlynn Mendes

After weeks of national discussions about women and girls' safety, the term "rape culture" has made headlines again. This time it relates to widespread reports of sexual violence against teenagers in secondary education, some of which include Britain's most prestigious fee-paying schools.

The revelations came after Everyone's Invited, a website and Instagram page dedicated to giving students a platform to report cases of sexual abuse and harassment, became inundated with testimonies in recent days.

Many girls who've spoken up have demanded that sexual violence and gender inequality be openly discussed and tackled by school leaders, while MPs have called for an inquiry.

Yet it seems there's an emerging argument that the real issue is not an ingrained culture of unhealthy sexual attitudes but how much exposure teenagers have to pornography and explicit images. As scholars investigating these issues, we've looked into the role that issues like unchallenged rape culture and online explicit materials play in influencing these harmful behaviours.

Student protests over sexual violence show how urgently schools should tackle these issues. Young people's online and offline lives are inseparably intertwined, and it's important to deliver relationships and sex education within this context. This means focusing not only on young people's digital interactions but what they do offline as well.

Rape culture and teens' everyday lives

Rape culture "condones, excuses, tolerates and normalises" sexual violence. Although feminists have been referring to rape culture since the 1970s, many have connected with the concept in recent years, particularly since the #MeToo movement. Namely, because it helps people understand toxic sexual behaviours and how they've been normalised in society at large – and in many schools.

For young people, rape culture is, unfortunately, part of everyday life and it's increasingly perpetuated online. As shared on Everyone's Invited, for example, girls are sometimes coerced online into sharing nude images of themselves. Not only are they harassed by partners and peers into sending these photos, but they receive them too. Other examples include girls receiving unwanted sexual messages via personal messaging services and social media.

Our UK survey of 336 young people in 2020 found that 32% of girls said they'd received a photo of a penis that they didn't want. Also called "cyberflashing", this increased during lockdown, and is often a gateway to more violence and abuse.

While mainstream internet porn can also perpetuate rape culture due to its tendency to promote harmful narratives like rape scenarios and generally sexist content, it's too easy to scapegoat it as the main cause of sexualised violence.

Sex education is also relevant here. The government's updated relationships and sex education guidance for the new curriculum in England encourages schools to emphasise relationships and sex education to children, while underlining the negatives of porn.

But as we've noted elsewhere it includes no advice to help teachers cover these issues, or information about why it's important to do so. Instead of just condemning internet porn, young people need education about sexual consent online and offline from an early age so they have the tools and resilience to manage sexual dynamics and scenarios.

The government also needs to invest in sex education that focuses on gender equality. A start in the right direction is the UK Council for Internet Safety's recent guidance on "sharing nudes and semi-nudes", which acknowledges how pervasive intimate image-sharing is among young people.

If government policy is going to continue to prioritise relationships and sex education, the new curriculum has to deal with some difficult issues, including how school lessons

should tackle the issue of sexual violence. Separately, to discourage a culture of silence in education, there also needs to be a review of schools with a history of covering up sexual abuse by pupils. Any attempt to meaningfully address these issues must work constructively with schools, rather than demonising them.

As researchers and as a sex education organisation, we've worked closely with safeguarding leads, who are the educators responsible for ensuring the safety of children both online and offline in secondary schools. They've shown a strong desire to find constructive ways to deal with the growing problem of image-based sexual abuse among students. Chiefly, they lamented schools' reactive and slow responses about these issues and spoke of how overwhelmed teachers were by the sheer volume of cases.

Without specific plans about how to deal with online sexual harassment more generally, these educators had to use existing internet, e-safety or anti-bullying policies to guide their often piecemeal response to complex incidents among students. We developed guidance on online sexual harassment to try and help.

Sex education in the digital era

In the work we do with young people and the sex education charity, School of Sexuality Education (SSE), we advocate for digital literacy as "the fourth pillar of education, alongside reading, writing and maths". Although young people are often considered "digital natives", platforms and technologies constantly change, and young people need training to safely navigate these spaces.

We know from our research that many teachers find it hard to keep up to date - they may have heard of the platforms young people use, but don't know how they function, or why some might present more risks and harms. They might not be aware of the fact that Snapchat, for example, is one of the worst platforms for cyberflashing, with our "staying safe online" survey revealing that 62% of unwanted sexual content was received there.

Teens also need spaces to understand and unpack gendered sexual expectations and double standards. Identifying who's most commonly targeted with notions like slutshaming – when people, namely women and girls, are criticised for being perceived to be overly sexual – could give people a chance to reflect on how they support existing inequalities. Sometimes that's all it takes to change a person's behaviour.

These conversations need to take place in non-judgemental environments, in which all young people feel safe and able to ask questions. And critically, the positive messages we teach in class must be echoed across all schools, including re-thinking how children's rights and consent can be promoted in everyday life, and what could threaten that progress. These forms of education aren't just vital for today's issues, but are pathways to recovery in the future.

31 March 2021

Sex sells, right?

The world is changing, and brands who found their fame by using sex in the past risk alienating consumers if they fail to keep up with evolving attitudes. Michaela Jefferson discovers how advertisers are embracing the challenge.

By Michaela Jefferson

"**S**ex sells" is probably the most famous cliche in advertising. Sex sells lingerie, sex sells jeans, sex sometimes even sells sparkling water, hearing aids and cat food.

But within the last 50 years, sex has catapulted some brands - Calvin Klein, Abercrombie & Fitch and Wonderbra, for example - into the mainstream. Others, like Levi's, have used sex to bring their businesses back to life.

However, despite being infamously repressed and tight-lipped about what goes on behind closed doors, perceptions of sex among British consumers have evolved enormously. With the likes of *Skins*, *Sex Education* and *50 Shades of Grey*, mainstream media has become so saturated with sex that *Game of Thrones* throwing incest into the mix barely raised an eyebrow.

Meanwhile, following Protein World's controversial "Are You Beach Body Ready?" ad in 2016, the Advertising Standards Authority (ASA) has been cracking down on

advertisers who sexually objectify men and women in their messaging. In December 2018, the ASA advised advertisers that "sexualisation and gratuitous nudity in ads can often cause serious or widespread harm and offence", and said that advertisers should avoid using sexualised imagery if it is "irrelevant" to the product.

So, with that in mind, can sex still have the selling power for advertisers that it once did?

"Ultimately? Yes and no," Jem Fawcus, CEO of brand strategy partner and insight agency Firefish, tells Mediatel.

"Every well observed element of human life can sell if used in the right way. But if used just for titillation and as an attention grabber, absolutely not."

First of all, brands need to be honest with themselves about whether or not they have "permission" to use sex appeal and sexuality in their communications, he says, as some sectors have more permission than others.

But even brands who found their fame by using sex in the past risk alienating consumers if they fail to keep up with evolving attitudes.

Calvin Klein, for example, came under heavy criticism this month for "queerbaiting" - faking a same-sex romance or attraction to attract an LGBT+ fan base - by releasing an ad in which supermodel Bella Hadid (who, crucially, identifies as straight) is depicted kissing the virtual influencer Lil Miquela.

And Victoria's Secret, the communication strategy of which has always revolved around portrayals of sex appeal, is another brand which has fallen foul of changing consumer sentiment.

"[Victoria's Secret's] is a sector you would expect to have every excuse to use sex, but it hasn't done it very well," Fawcus says.

"It's stayed as mainly women dressed up pretty much as objects, rather than evolving to reflect all the different facets that sex, sexuality and sex appeal can now encompass. The different gender depictions, the different roles."

The Victoria's Secret Fashion Show, the highlight of the lingerie brand's calendar year, has recently drawn criticism both for perpetuating unrealistic body standards and for refusing to represent segments of its market, including disabled, transgender and plus-size women.

Fatally, former CMO Ed Razek last year said he could not see trans-women ever being included in the show as it would ruin the "fantasy". This narrow interpretation of the boundaries of sexual fantasy caused outrage and, tellingly, Victoria's Secret is facing serious financial difficulties.

The brand's comparable sales are in continual decline, with 2018 sales down 8%; shares are trading at $22, a five year low; and in March, the brand announced that it would be closing 53 stores in the US. Meanwhile, market share has sunk from 31.7% in 2013 to 24% in 2018, according to the latest US women's underwear report from Coresight Research.

On the other hand, there are a number of new brands, run by women, which use sexual depictions of the female body in their communications and are thriving, including Fenty Beauty, Kylie Cosmetics and KKW. According to Fawcus, these brands have more permission to use sexualised imagery in their ads because the women behind them (Rihanna, Kylie Jenner and Kim Kardashian, respectively) are themselves "empowered".

"It's less about objectification and attention grabbing and more about these women expressing themselves in ways they feel comfortable with and that other people can feel comfortable with," he says, adding that as long as sex is used as "something people can relate to", that is funny or provokes conversation, "that works really well still".

In agreement, Malin Herrstrom, strategy director at Goodstuff Communications, says that whilst sex is "obviously" not suited to all products, it can be effective for some.

"Sex appeal doesn't need to be defined by the chiselled, oiled up bodies of strangers – it's about the empowering qualities and quirks of the individual," she says, praising brands like ASOS Face + Body and Nike Dream Crazier for playing to a "21st century definition" of sex appeal and "successfully separating sexy from sexist".

Other brands that have updated their definitions of sex appeal to fit a 21st century definition include some of the most overtly sexual (and retrospectively, sexist) advertisers of all time.

Wonderbra swapped out its "Hello Boys" billboard - which was once voted the most iconic ad of all time - for "Hello Me", a play on the original slogan to refocus on female empowerment and self love.

American Apparel - which ultimately had to file for bankruptcy after a series of scandals over its use of seemingly-underage models in sexually suggestive poses - relaunched online in 2018 with a racially and body diverse cast of adult models who are intended to look sexy, without being scantily clad. The brand is re-opening its first store this year.

And men's deodorant brand Lynx stopped suggesting that its product could attract swarms of bikini-clad women after sales began to freefall, and instead celebrates all facets of masculinity in its "Find Your Magic" campaign, which rejects the idea of conventional attractiveness and suggests that men are most attractive when they are confident in themselves.

"By adopting a more extensive definition [of sex appeal], brands can build cultural relevancy and display a better understanding and authentic connection with their consumers," Herrstrom says.

Male brain vs female brain

For brands who do want to use sex or titillation in their marketing campaigns it's also worth considering how consumers respond to sexual advertising on a neurological level, with attitudes to sex often differing from brain to brain.

According to Neuro-Insight, a neuromarketing and analysis company, men and women have very different neurological responses to the use of sex in advertising, largely due to the way we are "culturally conditioned" to view sex in society.

In a study that recorded the neurological responses of male and female brains towards three different ads that employ sexual themes or titillation - Wrigley's Extra's "Time to Shine", Lloyd Bank's "The M Word" and Original Source's "Original Source x Made in Chelsea" - on average women expressed higher levels of engagement.

Engagement, or personal relevance, is a key driver of long-term memory encoding, which is essential for the success of an ad as it has direct links to brand recall and future purchase decisions. For the Lloyds ad, average engagement was 19% higher for women.

However, although women related better to the content, on an emotional level their brains tended to withdraw - suggesting overall dislike. According to Neuro-Insight, this

is because the feeling they were relating to was the sense of awkwardness the actors are expressing around the topic of sex.

Meanwhile, men responded more positively on an emotional level, suggesting they found the ads more entertaining overall. Men showed over 60% higher levels of approach than women during the Original Source ad at the point when Made in Chelsea star Sam Thompson's clothes were stolen, which Neuro-Insight says is because they enjoyed the humour.

Despite this, low levels of personal relevance mean the ads did not code as effectively into memory as they did for women.

"We know there are cultural, contextual differences between the lives of men and women - that's natural," says Shazia Ginai, Neuro-Insight's CEO.

"Because of the cultural context in which we live, our brains will choose to take in or find relevance or have emotional responses to things a bit differently."

Sex will always have a place in advertising, as it is topical and relevant to consumers, she says. However, advertisers have to be "a little bit smarter" about how they communicate when targeting specific audiences.

"When you're targeting for something specific, remember that and take into account the fact that the tone of the sexual content or the tone of the suggestive content will be taken in two different ways."

A higher purpose

So for brands who have permission and who do it well, industry experts remain confident that sex still has power for advertisers.

However, Marie Oldham, chief strategy officer at VCCP Media, says that the "macro trends" for advertising are towards "authenticity, sustainability and engagement" as brand builders - so for advertisers selling products not directly linked to sex, finding another purpose for their brand will likely be more effective.

Mixers brand Fever-Tree in the 1970s may have featured "lovely" ladies preparing G&Ts for their "hard working" husbands, Oldham says, but now the brand is backing the global fight against Malaria.

Meanwhile, Cadbury - which was behind some of the most sexually provocative advertising of all time with its campaigns for Cadbury Flake - now focuses on portraying stories of human kindness.

"Sex will always sell," Oldham adds. "But fortunately for us, brands are finding more meaningful and sustainable platforms on which to build."

23 May 2019

Sex in advertising: does it still sell?

Is sex in advertising still an effective strategy? Or have we lost our mojo?

"**S**ex sells" – a phrase we all know too well. A statement of fact and passive acceptance. A concept that infiltrated the advertising industry nearly 134 years ago and has since been considered the norm.

Until now…

What exactly is sex in advertising?

I'm glad you asked…

Sex in advertising is the use of erotic or sexually provocative imagery, subliminal messages, or sounds designed to rouse consumer interest in a brand, product, or service.

If I tasked you to think of an ad that portrays a lovely lady or handsome fellow, my guess is it wouldn't take you long. Because despite sometimes tenuous links to the product or brand, sexualised marketing has been and is a proven method of luring in consumers.

But why?

History of sexualised advertisements

It goes back to basic, primal instincts. Alongside food, water, sleep, and general survival, sex (or the urge to procreate) lies amongst our interests of self-preservation.

But it's also about sensual pleasure – ain't no denying that! It moves beyond the physical to the psychological. To experiencing love, affection and ecstasy.

So, it's no surprise sexual imagery is a powerful tool and has been used as such for so long. It's capitalising on an innate, human disposition we respond to.

It all started in 1885, when a cigarette manufacturer began including erotic images, in the form of trading cards, in their packaging. The showcasing of the day's most esteemed female stars and the, I presume, allusion to "cigarettes after sex" worked. And worked well.

An avalanche of both suggestive and shameless sexual imagery has since cascaded into the advertising industry and brands will stop at nothing (bar censorship laws and regulations) to link their product, wherever they can, to sex.

While the arguable abuse of the concept increases, we can't deny the facts: sex sells.

Advantages of sex in advertising

This could be easily summed up in three words: dollar, dollar bills.

But that's only where the brand is concerned.

Men's magazines, such as FHM and Maxim, found that sexy ladies on their front covers outperformed images of male stars, regardless of whether said star was hot in the press at the time. A viewer will generally spend more time "viewing" the ad if it's sexually appealing, resulting in more sales. That's not to say I condone the use of such images – don't shoot the messenger.

There are sadly, and perhaps unsurprisingly, very few good examples of sexualised marketing that we can pull from, but it's worth a shot.

Heineken's Premature Pour campaign makes for an entertaining watch and saw an immediate 13% rise in sales. The implicit yet direct sexual nature of the ad shows how easy it becomes to incorporate humour into a sexualised advertisement (I certainly had a chuckle), thus increasing audience interest.

Durex obviously uses sex in advertising – they're a condom brand, for crying out loud. But their $2.50 > $217 is a great example of how to use sex in advertising, the right way.

It's funny, clever, and a gentle reminder to practice safe sex. #NoLoveWithoutAGlove

Hedkandi's Love What You See ad is a refreshing take on what we so often see in the advertising industry: sex pressuring women to look a certain way and men to expect certain "standards". Instead, here we have a woman who is looking the best for herself, rather than for anyone else. On the other hand, I'd argue whether a woman has to be size zero (like the model) to love herself, but that's for another post.

The problem with "sex sells"

Sex: it's naughty, it's taboo. We're not supposed to talk about it. So, when something is presented as "risqué", how do we respond?

Well, overtly we might say: "Oh, stop!" While our internal dialogue goes something along the lines of: "Don't stop…"

But before you get carried away looking for bouncy boobs to promote your new range of pots and pans, there are two things to consider here:

1. Sex can't sell everything. There has to be a context, and a relevant one at that.
2. We are starting to talk about sex. And using women's bodies to sell products has not only started to become more transparent, but it's actually turning people off.

Remember that humans are an intelligent species. They soon discover when they're being manipulated. And, in many cases, when a female body is being exploited.

A fine line exists when using sex in advertising, and brands are crossing it all too often.

A couple of examples come to mind: Dolce & Gabbana's Submissive Woman; Sprite's charming, slut-shamer of a Brutally Refreshing campaign; Protein World's Beach Body Ready billboards, to name a few.

But nothing – and I mean nothing – is as bad as Belvedere's "Unlike some people, Belvedere goes down smoothly", in which the brand thought it appropriate to make light of rape and sexual assault.

Sexual imagery may indeed attract a certain demographic, but the majority – especially nowadays – aren't buying it. If you're going to use sex in your advertising, ensure the strategy checks out and doesn't cross the line from sexual to sexist, or funny to offensive.

Does sex sell anymore?

I think sex in advertising can work and can continue to do so.

I don't think it's wrong to pair the two or think it indecent to do so. It just needs to make sense when it's done. Brands need to think about the product they're selling and the ways in which it relates to sex, without it being offensive and harmful.

If an ad is promoting warped body image, objectification, and/or sexism – or if it's simply clutching at an uninspired, dubious link between sex and the product – it's a guaranteed no-go.

I would encourage conversations about sex to be more open and free-flowing and I would personally love to see more sex-positive advertisements out there. Because many of us like to have sex, but nobody likes being objectified.

Does sex sell? Yes. But only when it's done the right way.

18 October 2019

German athlete Sarah Voss praised for wearing bodysuit to protest sexualisation of female gymnasts

Gymnast says she wants to show younger female athletes how they can present themselves aesthetically in a different form of clothing without feeling uncomfortable.

By Olivia Petter

German gymnast Sarah Voss has been praised for taking a stand against the sexualisation of female athletes by choosing to wear a full bodysuit at the 2021 European Artistic Gymnastics Championships in Basel, Switzerland.

Typically, female gymnasts are told to wear leotards for competitions that can either be half or long-sleeved.

A full bodysuit like the one Ms Voss chose to wear are seldom worn by women at competitions.

However, Team Germany has since confirmed on Twitter that Ms Voss's decision to wear one was to protest the way in which female athletes are often sexualised through their outfits.

The team shared in a statement on Twitter via the European Gymnastics account, saying:

"Our girls want to be role models for young gymnasts and show them how they can present themselves differently without feeling uncomfortable about certain elements."

Additionally, the German Gymnastics Association shared an image of Ms Voss on Twitter confirming that her choice to wear the bodysuit was a protest against the sexualisation of female athletes.

Ms Voss spoke about her decision to wear a bodysuit on her own Instagram page alongside a series of photographs of her competing in the outfit.

In the caption, Ms Voss wrote that she was "immensely proud" to wear the garment and explained that it made her "feel good" and "still look elegant".

Many people praised the gymnast for taking the initiative, with one fan writing: "This is awesome, love the uniform update, thanks for pushing for change in the sport!"

Another person tweeted: "It's revolutionary in so many ways to see Sarah Voss wear a leotard with legs at the European championships! Thank you Sarah for setting an example that aesthetics do not have to come at the expense of potential exposure and discomfort."

22 April 2021

Offence: sexualisation and objectification

Note: This advice is given by the CAP Executive about non-broadcast advertising. It does not constitute legal advice. It does not bind CAP, CAP advisory panels or the Advertising Standards Authority.

On 14 December 2018, CAP announced the introduction of a new rule on gender stereotyping in ads, and on 14 June 2019, Code rules 4.9 (CAP Code) and 4.14 (BCAP Code) were introduced. This rule states that ads 'must not include gender stereotypes that are likely to cause harm, or serious or widespread offence'. This followed a review of gender stereotyping in ads by the ASA and is also supported by additional guidance on potentially harmful gender stereotypes.

The rulings referenced below were published before the new rules came into force and so will not reference these rules, however the advice below still applies and should be read alongside the new guidance on depicting gender stereotypes likely to cause harm or serious or widespread offence.

The ASA receives many complaints about the depiction of women in a sexual or objectifying way in advertising, and in recent years the ASA has also received a number of complaints about ads that sexualise men, or portray men as objects, though these remain in the minority.

The ASA has a strong position on ads which may sexualise, or objectify people and advertisers must also ensure that ads do not present harmful or offensive gender stereotypes.

Sexualisation

Whilst depicting people in a sexual way is not always offensive or problematic, sexualisation and gratuitous nudity in ads can often cause serious or widespread harm and offence.

Advertisers should avoid using sexualised imagery if this is irrelevant to the product, as this is likely to be considered offensive. In 2016 the ASA investigated an ad for a fast food company which featured two images of a woman wearing only underwear, a jacket and trainers. One image featured the woman sitting on the edge of the sofa with her cleavage emphasised, her hands between her legs and her mouth open in what appeared to be a sexual pose. As this sexualised image of a woman bore no relevance to the advertised product, the ASA considered that the ad objectified women and was likely to cause serious offence. (Harlequin Fast Food, 12 October 2016).

Using animation or fictional concepts is unlikely to get marketers off the hook; in 2013 the ASA upheld a complaint about an ad for propeller "stripper" featuring an illustration of a topless mermaid (Ambassador Marine Ltd, 24 July 2013).

If the use of nudity is relevant to the advertised product the ASA is less likely to uphold complaints; toiletries and lingerie are good examples sef products for which nudity is likely to be acceptable. However, marketers should not take that to mean all risqué ads for those types of products will be acceptable. An ad for Playboy which appeared on public transport was considered to be overtly sexual, and likely to cause serious or widespread offence for featuring overtly sexual images of women in an untargeted medium. (Playboy TV UK Ltd, 07 November 2012).

Ads featuring suggestive or sexualised imagery of children, such as children in heavy make-up or provocative poses, are always problematic and should not be used. On 2 January 2018 Code rules 4.8 and 4.4 were added to the CAP and BCAP Codes respectively. These rules state that ads should not portray or represent in a sexual way anyone who is, or seems to be, under 18 years old. This does not apply to ads whose principal function is to promote the welfare of, or to prevent harm to, under18s, provided any sexual portrayal or representation is not excessive.

Objectification

Marketers should take care that depictions in ads do not objectify people. Objectification and sexualisation often overlap, and the ASA receives regular complaints in which women are objectified in a sexualised way.

Focussing on women's bodies while obscuring their faces is likely to be seen as objectifying women. A complaint about a VOD ad for Femfresh bikini line products was upheld by the ASA for being overly sexualised in a way that objectified women, because the ad featured sexualised dance moves, the clothes were revealing and the ad focused on the women's crotches with relatively few shots of their faces (Church & Dwight UK Ltd t/a Femfresh, 12 July 2017). Similarly, in 2013 the ASA upheld a complaint about an online ad for a car featuring women dancing in burlesque style lingerie. It noted that the ad featured a number of shots of the women's breasts and bottoms, but that their heads were obscured, and considered that this invited viewers to view the women as sexual objects. (Renault UK Ltd, 17 July 2013).

Whilst the majority of complaints are about the objectification of women, no one should be objectified in ads. Earlier this year the ASA upheld a complaint about an ad for an estate agency which pictured a man's torso and stated "WOW, WHAT A PACKAGE", and further text covering his crotch, because they considered that the ad was likely to have the effect of objectifying the man by using his physical features to draw attention to an unrelated product (Lewis Oliver Estates Ltd, 11 July 2018).

Innuendo and humour

Innuendo that is intended to be light-hearted can be acceptable but degrading language or visuals can offend, even if intended to be humorous. A radio ad for an electrical store in which the voiceover stated "Yes, everyone's going to Budd Electrical! It's B, U, double D and we all love a double D, right? ..." was ruled against by the ASA in 2016. Whilst the ad did not contain any nudity and was not overtly sexual presented women as sexual objects by inviting listeners to focus on their bra size, which was also unrelated to the service. (Budd Electrical Ltd, 07 September 2016). Similarly

a complaint about an ad for wine which featured a cropped image of a woman's torso accompanied by the text "taste the bush" was upheld by the ASA because the combination of concealing her face and the reference to her genitalia and oral sex was considered sexual objectification (Budge Brands Ltd t/a Premier Estates Wine, 04 November 2015).

Marketers should take care not to depict people in demeaning, subservient, exploitative, degrading or humiliating ways because such approaches are likely to cause serious or widespread offence.

13 August 2020

Sexually objectifying women leads women to objectify themselves, and harms emotional well-being

THE CONVERSATION

An article from The Conversation.

By Peter Koval, Elise Holland, Michelle Stratemeyer

How does a woman feel when a man wolf-whistles at her from across the street? Or when a male coworker gives her body a fleeting once-over before looking her in the eye?

These examples may seem relatively innocent to some, but our research has found they can have negative consequences for women's emotional well-being.

We asked women to record any incidents of sexual objectification on a smartphone app, alongside rating their feelings several times each day for a week.

When women experienced sexual objectification, in many cases it led them to scrutinise their physical appearance, which negatively impacted their emotional well-being.

A cycle of objectification

The process by which sexual objectification is psychologically harmful to women was first described by psychologists Barbara Fredrickson and Tomi-Ann Roberts in the mid-1990s.

According to this theory, when women are treated as objects, they momentarily view their own bodies from the perspective of the person objectifying them. In turn, they become preoccupied with their physical appearance and sexual value to others.

This process of "self-objectification" leads women to experience unpleasant feelings such as shame and anxiety. If repeated, it can eventually lead to long-term psychological harm.

Despite hundreds of studies on the psychology of sexual objectification, convincing evidence of the process described by Fredrickson and Roberts has been lacking until now.

We believe our research, conducted with colleagues in the United States, is the first to demonstrate that when women are exposed to sexually objectifying events in their everyday lives, they become more preoccupied with their physical appearance.

This, in turn, leads to increased negative emotions like anxiety, anger, embarrassment and shame.

Our research

We asked 268 women aged 18 to 46 in Melbourne and St Louis (in the US) to install an app on their smartphones.

Several times each day, the app prompted them to rate their emotions, how preoccupied they were with their physical appearance (a measure of self-objectification), and whether they had recently been targeted by sexually objectifying behaviour – or had witnessed such treatment of other women.

Using smartphones to track women's everyday experiences of sexual objectification has several advantages over other approaches used in most previous objectification research.

We asked women to document any incidents of sexual objectification in a smartphone app over a week.

First, we can be sure we captured "real world" examples of sexual objectification rather than artificial scenarios that may not represent life outside the lab.

Second, instead of relying on potentially unreliable memories of past events and feelings recorded in surveys or journals, by using frequent smartphone surveys we could gather more accurate "real time" reports of sexual objectification.

Finally, repeatedly sampling women's daily experiences enabled us to observe the psychological processes triggered by sexual objectification.

What we found

More than 65% of women in our study were personally targeted by sexually objectifying behaviour at least once during the monitoring period. This might have included being ogled, catcalled or whistled at.

Our findings were consistent with Fredrickson and Roberts's theory: women reported being preoccupied with their physical appearance roughly 40% more when they had recently been targeted by sexually objectifying behaviours, compared to when they had not.

Importantly, these momentary spikes in self-objectification predicted subsequent increases in women's negative emotions, particularly feelings of shame and embarrassment.

Although these increases were small, they were reliable, and appear to be indirectly caused by exposure to sexually objectifying behaviours.

Women may think about their appearance independent of experiencing sexual objectification. Interestingly, we found when women self-objectified, they sometimes reported feeling slightly happier and more confident.

So when women think about themselves in an objectified manner, they can feel both positive and negative emotions. But self-objectification that arises as a result of being objectified by someone else appears to have an exclusively negative impact on emotions.

It's important to note that in our results, experiencing sexual objectification on its own didn't directly lead to increases in women's negative feelings. Rather, the harmful effects of sexual objectification occurred when it resulted in women objectifying themselves.

Seeing other women objectified

Our participants reported witnessing the objectification of other women on average four times during the week-long study period.

Witnessing the objectification of other women was also followed by reliable (albeit weaker) increases in self-objectification, with similar negative downstream consequences for emotional well-being.

Just as passive smoking is harmful to non-smokers, second-hand exposure to sexual objectification may reduce the emotional well-being of women, even if they are rarely or never objectified themselves.

Overall, our study confirms previous research showing sexual objectification of women remains relatively common.

But importantly, we've shown these everyday objectifying experiences are not as innocuous as they may seem. Though subtle, the indirect emotional effects of objectifying treatment may accumulate over time into more serious psychological harm for women.

This article is a co-publication with Pursuit.

What is porn?

Pornography or 'porn' usually means videos and photos showing naked people or people engaged in sexual acts. Some people might look at porn as a way to learn about sex but it can have a damaging effect on their lives and relationships if they think it's realistic.

Does everybody watch porn?

No not everyone is watching porn, even if a lot of people say they are. It's OK to not want to watch it. It's definitely not something people have to do or feel pressured to do.

So what's the problem?

Porn can make you feel under pressure to look or behave a certain way. Most people wouldn't like it if you treated them the way people are treated in a porn film. Chances are, it wouldn't score you points with your partner. Watching it can make you think what they're doing is normal and that everyone would like it. But everyone is different, and what porn shows often isn't what happens in healthy and happy relationships.

Potential consequences of porn

If someone watches porn, they could develop unrealistic expectations.

Some people might start treating their sexual partner like somebody in a porn film, and expect them to do the things they've seen that don't happen in real life. This can make their partner feel pressured to look or act in a certain way and even be physically harmed. These are signs of an abusive relationship.

Even without pressure from a partner, learning about sex from porn may make people think they have to look and act in an unrealistic way. They may feel pressured into doing things they don't want to, thinking it would make them a good girlfriend or boyfriend.

Some people who watch a lot of porn become addicted to it and worry about the effect this is having on their lives.

Is porn legal to watch?

Most porn isn't illegal to watch or share, but some types of porn are illegal and you could get into serious trouble with the law. For example:

- ◆ Degrading porn, which can include things like someone humiliating another person.

- ◆ Violent porn, includes scenes of rape or sexual assault.

- ◆ Revenge porn, when people post or share pictures or videos that they took privately with, or received from a partner to humiliate them and have a negative impact on their lives.

- ◆ It's illegal to have, share or look at indecent or sexual images of children. Even if the images show people of a similar age to you, and you think they have given you permission to look at it, if they're under the age of 18, it's illegal.

2020

Addicted to porn

Young male who contacted ChildLine about being addicted to porn.

I first saw porn when I was eight. Lads at my primary school would show me videos and photos on their phones. It was a laugh and I wanted to join in. I then looked at it online and was shocked at how many sites came up in my online search. When I first properly watched it I looked at the images between my fingers as I was confused. After a while though it felt normal and I started enjoying it.

By secondary school I was accessing porn loads of times every day. At school, me and my friends would share them on our phones; none of the boys were embarrassed about watching it. At home, I watched it more and more in my room and was masturbating a lot too.

I downloaded films and images to my phone and watched adult TV channels. I knew all the channel numbers by heart and knew which channels had the best girls.

I hadn't known anything about sex before watching porn so learnt everything from there. I didn't understand about consent, how old people have to be able to give consent, or what was legal or not. I didn't know the positive and negative things about sex, all I knew was porn. I understand now that watching so much porn led me to have an unhealthy relationship with sex and the differences between porn sex and real sex.

Working with the NSPCC has helped me to understand what a healthy sexual relationship is, and how porn can mislead you to believing other things. The biggest thing I've learnt is about consent.

A couple of weeks ago one of my friends had a fight with his girlfriend because she wouldn't do things with him that he'd seen in porn. He thought it was ok to force her to do it. I got upset with him and defended his girlfriend.

I have a girlfriend now, and even though we're not old enough to be in a legal sexual relationship, when the time comes, it will be consensual and what both of us want. I respect her and her decisions and that's what being in a healthy relationship is.

I can't believe how much time I wasted on porn. I feel so much healthier by going out, playing football and going to the gym. I have a good relationship with my girlfriend. My message is there's more to life than porn and masturbating.

Disclaimer: All names and potentially identifying details have been changed to protect the identity of the young person.

2020

Porn use is up, thanks to the pandemic

An article from The Conversation.

THE CONVERSATION

By Joshua B. Grubbs Assistant Professor of Psychology, Bowling Green State University

Across the globe, the coronavirus pandemic is affecting almost all aspects of daily life. Travel is down; jobless claims are up; and small businesses are struggling.

But not all businesses are experiencing a downturn. The world's largest pornography website, Pornhub, has reported large increases in traffic – for instance, seeing an 18% jump over normal numbers after making its premium content free for 30 days for people who agree to stay home and wash their hands frequently. In many regions, these spikes in use have occurred immediately after social distancing measures have been implemented.

Why are people viewing more pornography? I'm a professor of clinical psychology who researches pornography use. Based on a decade of work in this area, I have some ideas about this surge in online pornography's popularity and how it might affect users in the long run.

What's the point of pornography?

People use pornography for a variety of reasons, but the most common reason is quite obvious: pleasure.

In 2019, my colleagues and I published a review of over 130 scientific studies of pornography use and motivation. We found that the most common reason people report for why they view pornography is sexual arousal. Research is abundantly clear that the majority of time that pornography is used, it is used as a part of masturbation.

Knowing that people use pornography to masturbate doesn't explain a great deal about why they might be using more pornography now.

My colleagues and I found that there are several additional reasons people might use pornography. For example, greater levels of psychological distress often predict higher levels of pornography use. People feeling lonely or depressed often report greater desire to seek out pornography; many people report using pornography to cope with feelings of stress, anxiety or negative emotions.

In short, people often turn to pornography when they are feeling bad, because pornography (and masturbation) likely offer a temporary relief from those feelings.

Psychology researchers also know that people use porn more when they are bored. I suspect this relationship between pornography use and boredom is quite likely one of those exponential functions that's been in the news so much in recent weeks. It's not just that more boredom predicts greater pornography use – extreme boredom predicts even higher levels of use. The more bored someone is, the more likely they are to report wanting to view pornography.

Is more pornography now a problem later?

The spread of the coronavirus and social distancing measures meant to help contain it have led to increases in social isolation, loneliness and stress – so increases in pornography use make sense.

But are there likely to be negative effects down the road?

Already, numerous anti-pornography activists have expressed grave concerns about these increases in use, with many groups providing resources for fighting those rises.

As a scientist, however, I'm skeptical of blanket claims that increased use right now will translate to widespread negative outcomes such as addiction or sexual dysfunction. Like most aspects of the ongoing coronavirus crisis, there are probably not enough data yet for researchers to make definitive predictions, but past studies do provide some ideas.

Generally speaking, most consumers do not report any problems in their lives as a result of pornography use. Among people who use pornography frequently – even every day – a large percentage report no problems from that use.

Some research, though, does find links between pornography use and potentially concerning outcomes. For example, for men, pornography use is often linked with lower levels of sexual satisfaction, but the current evidence doesn't untangle whether men use pornography more when they are dealing with sexual dissatisfaction or if men using pornography more leads to more sexual dissatisfaction.

For women, the results are even more unclear. Some studies have actually found that pornography use is associated with more sexual satisfaction, whereas others have found that it is not associated with sexual satisfaction at all.

Studies related to pornography use and mental health have found that hours spent using pornography do not necessarily cause depression, anxiety, stress or anger over time. The same holds for sexual dysfunctions. Although there are cases of people who state that pornography led them to experience erectile dysfunction, large-scale studies have repeatedly found that mere pornography use does not predict erectile dysfunction over time.

A distraction at a boring, anxious time

There is certainly evidence that some people who use pornography also report having mental health concerns or sexual problems in their lives; so far, though, the evidence linking pornography to those things does not appear to be causal.

In short, porn does not seem to be causing widespread problems, and it is probably offering people a distraction from the boredom and stress of current events.

Despite the fact that, prior to COVID-19, 17 states introduced or passed legislation calling pornography use a public health crisis, public health professionals have argued that it really is not one, and I tend to agree. COVID-19, on the other hand, certainly is a public health crisis.

Although humanity has survived countless pandemics over the ages, the current one is the first to occur in the digital age. As disruptive as the coronavirus has been, for many people, opportunities for entertainment and distraction remain greater than they have been at any other point in history.

When social distancing measures are lifted and people are once again permitted to safely spend time with friends, strangers and potential sexual partners, I would expect that pornography use will return to pre-COVID-19 levels. For most users, pornography is probably just another distraction – one that might actually help "flatten the curve" by keeping people safely occupied and socially distanced. Combined with the fact that many people are isolating alone, pornography may provide a low risk sexual outlet that does not cause people to risk their own safety or the safety of others.

8 April 2020

Porn and children: the facts

We often come across RSE and PSHE resources which seem to have been written in the belief that 'sex education' means educating children about the types of porn that is available. We have seen pornography described as 'harmless', 'fun' and even 'empowering'. This is not backed up by the evidence.

We believe that good quality sex education should cover pornography, and should acknowledge that it is everywhere and that children may well have seen it. However it should also cover the harm that porn does, the way that its use affects relationships and both mental and physical health.

Here are some facts about pornography and how it effects children:

Porn – some statistics

2010:

An analysis of the content of porn films revealed:

♦ 88% of scenes included physical aggression such as gagging, choking, and slapping.

♦ In 94% of those scenes the aggression was directed towards women.

♦ Women were slapped in 75% of those scenes.

2015:

♦ 10% of 12 to 13-year-olds feared they were addicted to porn.

♦ More than four in 10 girls between the ages of 13 and 17 in England said they had been coerced into sex acts.

♦ 22% of schoolgirls reported suffering physical attacks, intimidation from their boyfriends, including slapping, punching and strangling.

2019

♦ 42 billion visits to Pornhub, up from 33.5 billion visits the previous year, or a 25% increase.

♦ 6.83 million new videos on Pornhub.

♦ Average daily visitors to Pornhub: 115 million, up 15 million a day from the year before – this figure exceeds the combined populations of Canada, Poland and New Zealand.

♦ 2.8 hours of new content uploaded every minute/ 4,032 hours of new content every 24 hours/ 1,471,680 hours of new content uploaded in 2019.

♦ 77,861 searches per minute or 1,297.6 searches per second.

A study of teenagers' porn viewing habits found that 75% of parents did not believe their children had ever seen pornography. However the majority of these parents' children told the researchers that they had viewed adult material.

Rachel Fitzsimmons, a sex educator who speaks to school children, said on *Women's Hour* that "nearly 100 per cent" of the boys she speaks to in schools have seen pornography and this is "how they learn about sex".

Lockdown

Figures that are available for lockdown show a drastic increase in Italy, where Pornhub offered its premium service for free. Consequently, Pornhub traffic increased by an enormous 57%; 4.3% behind Spain.

Many children now have access to the mobile technology that Pornhub credits for this increase. According to an article written for the Journal of Clinical Medicine, mobiles are part of what is known as the "triple-A" influences: accessibility,

Martellozzo added the concerns were not a "moral panic", and that she and others are working towards controlling what was available online.

"We can't of course generalise and say that everybody that watches porn would move on into wanting to act out what they had seen, but we do know that some young men do want to act out what they have seen and therefore expect girls to respond to their request, respond to their desire of performance," she said.

Dr Leila Frodsham, a consultant gynaecologist and spokesperson for the Royal College of Obstetricians and Gynaecologists, said there could be other consequences of young people watching porn." One knock-on effect that people might not consider is girls and women feeling their genitalia should look a certain way because that's what they have seen in the mass media or that's what boys are seeing through pornography and telling girls," she said.

"We are very concerned by reports that labiaplasty rates – surgery to change the look of the vagina – are increasing in under 18s, especially as there is no scientific reason to support its practice."

Experts agree better sex education is crucial. "What is needed is open, serious, honest conversations about sexual consent, about sex in relationships and about the broader context and the complexities [of sex]," McCormack said.

Martellozzo added there needed to be a shift in emphasis away from blaming victims of sexual harassment and abuse and instead a focus on perpetrators. "The emphasis here is really to educate the individual, and demonstrate to them that the effects of their choice of language or action is huge," she said.

Frodsham also stressed the need for better education. "Pornography provides children and young people with a false impression of what to expect when they do start having sex and can set unrealistic goals for boys and girls when it comes to exploring their sexuality," she said.

"It's widely disputed whether porn directly influences a rape culture. What is clear is that the matter of consent and what a healthy relationship looks like needs to be tackled head on in the school curriculum, so that boys and girls learn to respect one another and girls know to raise the alarm if they do experience abuse."

29 March 2021

In addition, he said research had found those who watch porn were not more sexist than those who did not. Where porn did cause problems, he said, it tended to be indirect, for example tensions with a partner owing to non-disclosure of porn-watching – it was not necessarily the case that those who watch porn then wished to act out what they saw.

"My concern when we go to porn as the problem, that just focuses on, in a sense, a technology and a thing, and not actually the much deeper and broader issues we need to address: sexual harassment, sexism, gender inequality," he said.

But others say pornography is problematic.

"Unfortunately the pornography that is widely available online can be graphic and aggressive, and the women depicted on some of the sites are getting younger and younger, borderline to being illegal," said Dr Elena Martellozzo, an associate professor in criminology at Middlesex University.

Martellozzo added that the message that men had a "right" to women's bodies undermined the notion of consent. "This is the definition of rape culture in a nutshell," she said.

According to research by Martellozzo and colleagues based on data collected in between 2015 and 2016 and published this year, 65% of 15- to 16-year-olds in the UK reported seeing pornography, with porn more commonly seen by boys.

Just over half of the 241 of boys in the study aged 11-16 who had seen porn said they thought it was "realistic" compared with 39% of 195 girls in the study who had seen porn with 44% of boys and 29% of girls saying it had given them ideas to try out.

We need to talk to our children about pornography – even if it makes us uncomfortable

Until we talk about how porn isn't a balanced representation of how sex should be enjoyed, we'll never change the culture that implies being sexually assaulted – and living in fear – is just part of being a woman.

By Shappi Khorsandi

We need to talk to our children about pornography. None of us want to, but we have to. And it can't wait until they are 17 – that's too late; not least because they are absolutely sure they know more than their parents about everything, long before this age.

Rampant "rape culture" in schools and higher education institutions has been uncovered via a website called Everyone's Invited, which asks people to call out sexism in schools across the UK via anonymous submissions.

Anonymous testimonials share experiences of sexual abuse – and a quick look through it had me in tears. So many were schoolchildren, mostly girls, being abused by other pupils.

Now, I'm not saying online pornography is solely to blame; obviously sexual assault happened before the internet was invented.

But even adults who didn't grow up with it can become obsessed and sucked into a world where sex is only gratifying if someone – usually a woman – looks like they are being forced, abused and in pain.

Add to that hideous mix our societal norm of "boys will be boys", and you get the attitude forming at a very tender age that sex is something boys want and girls have to give. It's

nothing new; parents need to talk to their children before they have a chance to go anywhere near porn. And they will watch it – we can't protect them from it until they are 18, it's impossible.

Until we properly open a conversation with our children about how pornography isn't a balanced representation of how sex should be enjoyed, we will never change the culture that implies that occasionally being sexually assaulted – and living in fear – is just part of being a woman.

Equally, not being given space to talk about the emotions around sex can also lead to harm. "Enthusiastic consent" was a concept that was verbalised to me fairly recently, when I confided in a friend that I was upset because I'd had sex with a boyfriend when I really wasn't in the mood – and only did it to stop him getting into a sulk about it.

I, a confident, grown woman, have found myself saying, "oh, for God's sake, go on then", and felt rotten about it afterwards, more times than I care to recall. You can know logically that sex isn't anyone's "right" to have, but still be guilt-tripped and pressurised into letting your body be used.

It's down to parents to educate their children about all this – and you simply can't without addressing porn.

In my day, being "kinky" meant you occasionally wore fishnet stockings and high heels during sex, and had a can of whipped cream to hand. These days, unless you are into whips, chains, hot wax, choking, slapping, spanking, scat (not the jazz kind) or dressing up, you're "vanilla" – and there is an infinite amount of porn content made to sate your desires which go beyond your own imagination.

This word, "vanilla", is used to diminish nice, sensual, gentle bonking with meaningful eye contact as "boring". Who wants to be boring? A quick survey of my younger friends concluded that whipped cream is strictly for pancakes and hot chocolate – and you'd no more bring whipped cream into bed than you would a floret of broccoli.

Swathes of pornographic content feed rape fetishists. Tags of "forced", "helpless" and "punished" pop up, uninvited. If you're a young teen looking at it as your first exposure to sex – and your parents have not spoken to you about what's out there – then it's easy to think that's what sex is, and that's what everyone does.

Don't get me wrong: there is nothing wrong with kinks between consenting adults. I'm in no position to judge anyone, believe me. But it is now utterly impossible to stop people seeing these images of women in porn being trussed up like turkeys, having a horrible time.

You can imagine how, if you don't have anyone to talk to about what you've seen, you might think that's the standard for everyone. When really, what we need to do is normalise talking about this stuff.

My son is almost 14, and I have talked to him about how in a lot of pornography, you stumble across things you can't "unsee". I've told him often the women are dehumanised and don't look like they are having a good time; and if he ever sees porn like that, to understand its danger.

These aren't long, earnest conversations. I try to be matter-of-fact and appropriate so as not to make him feel too awkward (but let's face it: it's going to be awkward; nobody wants to talk to their mum about porn – but that's still no reason not to). They discuss consent at his school, and I have talked to him about "enthusiastic" consent. Obviously, I don't want him watching porn; but he needs to know I am aware of it and what my values are around it.

Even if it's a one night stand we should be able to say (before we get into bed) what we are into and what we are not. Opening up conversations at home about sex and porn will make it easier to communicate and put down boundaries when we choose sexual partners.

Children are swayed by their parents' values above everything else. If your mum or dad call women "harlots" or "slutty" based on what they know, or think they know, about their individual sex lives then that's going to affect how you shape your own attitudes.

It feels crucial to me that I never use language which judges people in this way. It's important that neither of my children regard sex as something secret and "naughty", to hold any shame around.

And, any time they want to ask anything, they can – and know I will answer in an age appropriate way. The last thing we want is our children to learn about sex from Pornhub.

7 April 2021

Porn is not the root of all evil – yes, even when it comes to your children watching it behind your back

As a sociology professor, I've studied and conducted my own research about the myths parents have accepted. Let me tell you, adult entertainment isn't nearly as damaging as poor sex education.

By Mark McCormack

A new British Board of Film Classification (BBFC) study has found that British teenagers regularly watch porn, and that parents are unaware or in denial about it. Surprising? No. But the results do reveal something interesting about how readily we accept so many misconceptions about porn.

The survey, conducted as part of the BBFC and the government's now scrapped age verification "porn block" rollout, found that while porn is increasingly a source of education about sex, young people also discuss viewing material they found disturbing. As such, most parents support stricter online policing of porn to stop young children accidentally watching such material.

The fears that parents have about their children viewing porn are understandable.

Conversations between parents and children about sex are awkward and the issue of online porn combines this difficulty with concerns about the damaging effects porn has on young people. Yet the risks of porn are exaggerated, and responding by censoring it through technology will not address the underlying issues for young people or their parents.

As media reports on the study indicates, young people are watching porn without their parents knowing. My own research found that young people chose to watch porn and found ways around their parents' strategies to stop them. The problems they encountered related to their parents' punishments and not their porn consumption.

The theory of why porn is harmful is that consumers will start to adopt troubling aspects of it in their attitudes and behaviours. If porn objectifies women, is violent or contains rape myths, the theory is that these things will develop in the people that watch it. Young people, then, will start to objectify women more because of the availability of porn. Or, if porn is violent, they will believe violence is a standard part of sex.

But that's a limited and simplistic perspective of how people watch porn. It is a "monkey see, monkey do"

theory of consumption where people are passive consumers of a script that they entirely accept and then act out themselves. It is far easier to blame porn for young people's sexual interests than to recognize that young people are interested in sex.

The other key factor is that there is scant evidence for porn having this damaging impact. Exposure to online porn does not lead to risky sexual behaviours among young people. A systematic review of the impact of internet pornography on adolescents found that the evidence for correlations between porn consumption and a range of social and health outcomes were inconclusive, with little replicability across studies.

We are now almost inundated with research that counters the harmful porn narrative. Avid porn consumers who attend porn "expos" have more gender egalitarian views than the general population; porn addiction does not exist; online porn has not been getting more violent and people do not prefer violent porn in general. When young people seek out porn to watch, they tend to enjoy it and do not find it harmful.

Research is also now focusing on the potential benefits of watching porn. Just as the BBFC study reportedly finds young people watching porn as a form of sex education, research documents several educational benefits for young people: helping them understand their sexual identities, explore sexual fantasies in a safe environment, and educate themselves about sexual health.

That young people may be watching porn they feel disturbed by or being sent sexual images without their consent is far more troubling. Importantly, there is a lack of evidence for long-term harm caused by unintentionally watching porn or seeing porn that is disturbing. There is no evidence that young people who watch porn and dislike it continue to watch it.

The sharing of sexual images without consent requires a serious policy response, but given that it occurs mostly through messaging apps on smartphones, age verification systems aren't an appropriate response to that problem. What we need instead, is a sophisticated approach to educating young people about the risks of and responsibilities in sexting. It is wrong to conflate inappropriate sexting with the availability of online porn.

This is not to argue away the importance of talking about porn. If porn is now serving as the primary form of sex education for young people, that is an indictment of sex education in schools and how we speak to young people about sex more generally. The BBFC report identifies a chasm of understanding and practice between children and their parents, and that demands attention. Porn consumption can still be problematic, and the unwanted sharing of sexually explicit material requires educational and legal action.

But the response to these issues must be one that fosters communication and knowledge between young people and adults and improves sex education in schools that is currently failing young people. An age-verification system that has already proven to be unworkable will not stop young people watching porn and it will not educate them about sexual consent and safety online. We do not need a technological fix to the "problem" of porn, but an educational response to the reality that when it comes to talking openly and honestly about sex and sexuality, we have a serious problem, especially with young people.

Mark McCormack is a professor of Sociology in the Department of Social Sciences at the University of Roehampton

5 February 2020

Key Facts

- Sexualisation is an issue because it imposes adult sexuality and harmful sexual stereotypes on young people. (page 1)

- Research has also discovered links between sexualisation of young people and violence – sexualisation can lead to more acceptable attitudes to violence, increased sexual harassment and to child sexual abuse. (page 1)

- Gender stereotypes are a large part of the reason that one in six women is sexually assaulted, one in four women experience intimate partner violence, and more than one and a half million women were the victims of violent crime last year (2019). (page 3)

- Despite being the least successful group on dating apps, black women are widely desired on the basis of archaic, offensive sexual stereotypes (page 7)

- A UK survey of 336 young people in 2020 found that 32% of girls said they'd received a photo of a penis that they didn't want. Also called "cyberflashing", this increased during lockdown, and is often a gateway to more violence and abuse. (page 19)

- The government's updated relationships and sex education guidance for the new curriculum in England encourages schools to emphasise relationships and sex education to children, while underlining the negatives of porn. (page 19)

- Snapchat is one of the worst platforms for cyberflashing, A "staying safe online" survey revealed that 62% of unwanted sexual content was received there. (page 20)

- In December 2018, the ASA advised advertisers that "sexualisation and gratuitous nudity in ads can often cause serious or widespread harm and offence", and said that advertisers should avoid using sexualised imagery if it is "irrelevant" to the product. (page 21)

- According to Neuro-Insight, a neuromarketing and analysis company, men and women have very different neurological responses to the use of sex in advertising, largely due to the way we are "culturally conditioned" to view sex in society. (page 23)

- in 1885 a cigarette manufacturer began including erotic images, in the form of trading cards, in their packaging. The showcasing of the day's most esteemed female stars worked (to increase sales). (page 24)

- Men's magazines, such as *FHM* and *Maxim*, found that sexy ladies on their front covers outperformed images of male stars, regardless of whether said star was hot in the press at the time. (page 24)

- On 14 December 2018, CAP (Committeee of Advertising Practice) announced the introduction of a new rule on gender stereotyping in ads, and on 14 June 2019, Code rules 4.9 (CAP Code) and 4.14 (BCAP Code) were introduced. This rule states that ads 'must not include gender stereotypes that are likely to cause harm or serious or widespread offence'. (page 27)

- On 2 January 2018 Code rules 4.8 and 4.4 were added to the CAP and BCAP Codes respectively. These rules state that ads should not portray or represent in a sexual way anyone who is, or seems to be, under 18 years old. (page 27)

- Most porn isn't illegal to watch or share, but some types of porn are illegal and you could get into serious trouble with the law. (page 30)

- It's illegal to have, share or look at indecent or sexual images of children. Even if the images show people of a similar age to you, and you think they have given you permission to look at it, if they're under the age of 18, it's illegal. (page 30)

- In 2019 a review of over 130 scientific studies of pornography use and motivation was published. It found that the most common reason people report for why they view pornography is sexual arousal. (page 31)

- In 2019, there were 42 billion visits to Pornhub, up from 33.5 billion visits the previous year, or a 25% increase. (page 33)

- A study of teenagers' porn viewing habits found that 75% of parents did not believe their children had ever seen pornography. (page 33)

- NHS figures, reported on Radio 4 *Women's Hour* in 2019, revealed the number of teenagers in therapy for porn addiction had increased 228% in just two years, from 1400 to 4600. (page 34)

Glossary

Androgynous

Gender neutral, as opposed to appearing strictly male or female. Androgyny usually implies a blend of both feminine and masculine attributes.

Beauty pageant

Beauty pageants are generally aimed at females (though similar events do exist for males). Contestants are judged on the combined criteria of physical beauty, personality and talent. There is, however, a tendency to focus on physical appearance above other characteristics. Some feel that beauty pageants are inappropriate for young girls because they promote a nation obsessed with looks. On the other hand, some believe that pageants promote confidence and self-esteem.

Commercial/Commercialisation

Exploiting something in order to gain money.

Commercial sexual exploitation of children

The Declaration and Agenda for Action against Commercial Sexual Exploitation of Children defines this as a fundamental violation of children's rights. It comprises sexual abuse by the adult and remuneration in cash or kind to the child or a third person or persons. The child is treated as a sexual object and a commercial object. The commercial sexual exploitation of children constitutes a form of coercion and violence against children, and amounts to forced labour and a contemporary form of slavery. Commercial sexual exploitation of children may take the form of child abuse through the prostitution of children; using children to create images of child sex abuse (child 'pornography'); providing children to visitors from overseas for the purpose of sexual abuse (child sex tourism), and child marriage where a child is used for sexual purposes in exchange for goods or services. Children who are sexually exploited in these ways may have been trafficked from another country for that purpose.

Fetishisation

To have an excessive interest in or attraction to something.

Gender stereotypes

Simplifying the roles and attributes of and the differences between males and females. Gender stereotyping encourages children to behave in ways that are considered most typical of their sex. For example, buying pink toys for girls and blue for boys, or limiting girls to playing with dolls and boys to toy cars.

Grooming

Actions that are deliberately performed in order to encourage a child to engage in sexual activity. For example, offering friendship and establishing an emotional connection, buying gifts, etc.

Objectification

To reduce the status of a person – usually a female – to a mere object.

Pornification

Very similar to sexualisation, the term pornification refers to the acceptance of sexualisation in our culture.

Rape culture

An environment or culture that normalises sexual violence, trivialises sexual assault and tolerates sexual harrassment against (mostly) women. Rape culture often blames and shames victims while excusing the perpetrator.

Sexualise/Sexualisation

To give someone or something sexual characteristics and associations. This refers to the idea that sex has become much more visible in culture and media today. Premature sexualisation of children involves exposure to sexual images and ideas at an age when they are emotionally unable to process such information. Implications include children having sex at a younger age, engaging in activities such as sexting, and an increased likelihood of being groomed and it has been linked to hypermasculine behaviour in boys and young men.

Watershed restrictions

A television watershed is in place to protect children from viewing material that is inappropriate for their age group. Adult content can only be shown after a certain time (or 'after the watershed'). Some examples of adult content include graphic violence, nudity, swearing, gambling and drug use. Watershed times can vary around the world due to cultural difference. For example, in the UK the watershed for free-to-air television is between 21:00 and 05:30, whereas in the United States it begins at 22:00 and ends at 06:00.

Activities

Brainstorming

♦ What is meant by the term 'sexualisation'?

♦ Name some industries in which 'sexualisation' is a problem.

♦ How does sexualisation negatively impact young people's mental health?

♦ What is 'rape culture'?

Research

♦ Visit a selection of high-street stores or supermarkets that sell children's clothes. Make a note of anything you find for children aged 14 or under that you consider to be 'sexualised' or inappropriate for its target age-group. Take photographs if the store manager allows you to do so. Share your findings with the rest of your class.

♦ Over the course of one week, make a note of the adverts you see on television, online and in magazines/newspapers that might be considered to sexualise men or women. If possible, cut out the advert or take a photograph of it. At the end of the week, tally up how many sexualised adverts you've seen featuring men vs. how many featuring women. Create a simple bar graph to demonstrate your findings and share with your class.

♦ In pairs, search online for examples of sexualised imagery being used to sell:

- Dairy products
- Cars
- Soft drinks
- Clothes

Screenshot or print off what you have found and share with the rest of your class.

Design

♦ Choose one of the articles from this book and create an illustration that highlights the key themes of the piece.

♦ Design a leaflet that gives parents advice about how to talk to their children about pornography.

♦ As a class, stage a television talk show with the theme 'Should we teach pornography in schools?' The talk show panel should include a teacher, a politician, a parent and a journalist. One member of the class should also play the part of the talk show host, fielding questions from the audience as you debate the issue. Take some time to decide who will play each part, and think about what their opinion would be.

♦ Read the article on page 26: *German athlete Sarah Voss praised for wearing bodysuit to protest sexualisation of female gymnasts*. Think about other sports/activities where the attire for female athletes can make them vulnerable to sexualisation. Design a few alternative options.

Oral

♦ Do you think the rise in sexism and 'rape culture' in educational settings is directly related to increasingly easy access to pornography? Discuss in small groups and feed back to the rest of the class.

♦ Choose one of the illustrations from the book and consider what message your chosen picture is trying to get across. How does it support, or add to, the points made in the accompanying article? Do you think it is successful?

♦ In small groups, discuss why you think young people share nude selfies.

♦ In pairs, list all the examples of sexualisation you can think of. For example, perfume adverts, children's clothes, celebrities etc. When you've finished, compare with your classmates.

Reading/writing

♦ Is sexualisation in video games only linked to female characters? Write a blog post exploring your opinion. Aim to write at least 500 words but remember it is a blog and style your language accordingly.

♦ After reading some of the topic articles as a starting point, write your own definition of the term 'sexualisation'. When you have finished, split into small groups and discuss your definitions. Feed back to the rest of the class.

♦ Write a definition of the term 'objectification'.

♦ Write a definition of the term 'sexual harassment'.

♦ Write a blog post from either one of these two points of view, explaining why you feel the way you do:

- A mother who does not want her eleven-year-old daughter to wear make-up.
- A mother who allows her eleven-year-old daughter to wear make-up.

Index

A

advertising 21–25, 27–28

androgynous 41

avatars 6

B

beauty pageants 41

body image 3

body positivity 4

C

clothing

    age-appropriate 4

    and sexualisation 3, 11

commercial sexual exploitation of children 41

consent 3–4, 19, 31, 34–35, 37–38

cultivation hypothesis 6

Cuties 15–17

cyberflashing 19–20

D

dehumanisation 1

E

eating disorders 3

Eilish, Billie 11

empathy 6

F

fetishisation 7–8, 41

Framing Britney Spears 9–10

G

gaming 5–6

gender stereotypes 3, 20, 27–28, 41

grooming 41

H

hypersexualisation 3, 8

I

innuendo 28

L

labiaplasty 36

Lolita 16

Love Island 18

M

Madonna-Whore Complex 9

misogyny 12

N

non-contact abuse 34

nudity 17

O

objectification 1, 17–19, 27–29, 41

online safety 19–20

P

pornification 41

pornography 2, 30–39

    addiction to 31, 34

    damage from 30, 34–35

    and rape culture 34–36

    talking about 37–38

    and violence 30, 33

Q

queerbaiting 22

R

racism 7–8

rape 34

rape culture 19–20, 35–37, 41

'rape myths' 6

S

school skirts 12–13

self esteem 4

sex education 19–20, 36

sexism 6

sexual abuse 34–35

sexual assault 34–37

sexual harassment 19–20

sexualisation

    and advertising 21–25, 27–28

    of celebrities 9–11

    and clothing 3, 11

    definition 1, 41

    in gaming 5–6

    of men and boys 3, 17–19

    and skin colour 7–8

    in sport 26

    of teenagers 2–4, 12–14

    and violence 1, 3, 6

    of women and girls 3, 12–14, 18

    of young children 2–3

sexual violence 19–20

shaming 12–13, 20

skin colour 7–8

slavery 7

slurs 12–14, 20

social media 3

Spears, Britney 9–10

sport 26

stereotyping 1

    and gender 3, 27–28, 41

    and skin colour 7–8

superheros 2–3

T

teenagers, sexualisation of 2–3, 12–14

Timberlake, Justin 9

toxic masculinity 3

V

victim blaming 36

violence 1, 3, 6, 19–20

virginity 2, 9

Voss, Sarah 26

W

watershed restrictions 41

Acknowledgements

The publisher is grateful for permission to reproduce the material in this book. While every care has been taken to trace and acknowledge copyright, the publisher tenders its apology for any accidental infringement or where copyright has proved untraceable. The publisher would be pleased to come to a suitable arrangement in any such case with the rightful owner.

The material reproduced in ISSUES books is provided as an educational resource only. The views, opinions and information contained within reprinted material in ISSUES books do not necessarily represent those of Independence Educational Publishers and its employees.

Images

Cover image courtesy of iStock. All other images courtesy Freepik, except pages 9 & 11: Shutterstock.com

Illustrations

Simon Kneebone: pages 5, 21 & 30. Angelo Madrid: pages 2, 13 & 25.

Additional acknowledgements

With thanks to the Independence team: Shelley Baldry, Danielle Lobban, Jackie Staines and Jan Sunderland.

Tracy Biram

Cambridge, May 2021